# Bilingual
## VISUAL
# dictionary

# Bilingual

## VISUAL

# dictionary

Previously published as part of
*5-Language Visual Dictionary*

AURORA PUBLIC LIBRARY

## DK LONDON

Senior Editors Angeles Gavira, Christine Stroyan, Angela Wilkes
Senior Art Editor Ina Stradins
Jacket Editor Claire Gell
Jacket Design Development Manager Sophia MTT
Preproduction Producer Andy Hilliard
Producer Jude Crozier
Picture Researcher Anna Grapes
Managing Editor Dan Mills
Managing Art Editors Anna Hall, Phil Ormerod
Associate Publisher Liz Wheeler
Publisher Jonathan Metcalf

## DK INDIA

Editors Arpita Dasgupta, Shreya Sengupta, Arani Sinha
Assistant Editors Sugandha Agarwal, Priyanjali Narain
DTP Designers Harish Aggarwal, Ashwani Tyagi, Anita Yadav
Jacket Designer Juhi Sheth
Managing Jacket Editor Saloni Singh
Preproduction Manager Balwant Singh
Production Manager Pankaj Sharma

Designed for DK by WaltonCreative.com
Art Editor Colin Walton, assisted by Tracy Musson
Designers Peter Radcliffe, Earl Neish, Ann Cannings
Picture Research Marissa Keating

Language content for DK by g-and-w PUBLISHING
Managed by Jane Wightwick, assisted by Ana Bremón
Translation and editing by Christine Arthur
Additional input by Dr. Arturo Pretel, Martin Prill,
Frédéric Monteil, Meinrad Prill, Mari Bremón, Oscar Bremón,
Anunchi Bremón, Leila Gaafar

First American Edition, 2009
This edition published in the United States in 2017 by DK
Publishing, 345 Hudson Street, New York, New York 10014

Copyright © 2009, 2015, 2017 Dorling Kindersley Limited
DK, a Division of Penguin Random House LLC
17 18 19 20 21   10 9 8 7 6 5 4 3 2 1
001—306407—Apr/17

A catalog record for this book is available
from the Library of Congress.
ISBN: 978-1-4654-5929-9

DK books are available at special discounts when purchased
in bulk for sales promotions, premiums, fund-raising, or
educational use. For details, contact: DK Publishing Special
Markets, 345 Hudson Street, New York, New York 10014
SpecialSales@dk.com

Printed and bound in China

A WORLD OF IDEAS:
SEE ALL THERE IS TO KNOW

www.dk.com

# Inhalt
## contents

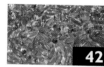

# die Menschen •
## people

# die äußere Erscheinung • appearance

# die Gesundheit •
## health

# das Haus • home

# die Dienstleistungen • services

# der Einkauf •
## shopping

# die Nahrungsmittel • food

deutsch • english

# über das Wörterbuch

Bilder helfen erwiesenermaßen, Informationen zu verstehen und zu behalten. Dieses zweisprachige Wörterbuch enthält eine Fülle von Illustrationen und präsentiert gleichzeitig ein umfangreiches aktuelles Vokabular in zwei europäischen Sprachen.

Das Wörterbuch ist thematisch gegliedert und behandelt eingehend die meisten Bereiche des heutigen Alltags, vom Restaurant und Fitnesscenter, Heim und Arbeitsplatz bis zum Tierreich und Weltraum. Es enthält außerdem Wörter und Redewendungen, die für die Unterhaltung nützlich sind und das Vokabular erweitern.

Dies ist ein wichtiges Nachschlagewerk für jeden, der sich für Sprachen interessiert – es ist praktisch, anregend und leicht zu benutzen.

### Einige Anmerkungen

Die zwei Sprachen werden immer in der gleichen Reihenfolge aufgeführt – Deutsch und Englisch.

Substantive werden mit den bestimmten Artikeln, die das Geschlecht (Maskulinum, Femininum oder Neutrum) und den Numerus (Singular oder Plural) ausdrücken, angegeben, zum Beispiel:

| **der Samen** | **die Mandeln** |
|---|---|
| seed | almonds |

Die Verben sind durch ein (v) nach dem englischen Wort gekennzeichnet:

**ernten** • harvest (v)

Am Ende des Buchs befinden sich Register für jede Sprache. Sie können dort ein Wort in einer der zwei Sprachen nachsehen und die jeweilige Seitenzahl nachsehen.
Die Geschlechtsangabe erfolgt mit folgenden Abkürzungen:

m = Maskulinum
f = Femininum
n = Neutrum

# die Benutzung des Buchs

Ganz gleich, ob Sie eine Sprache aus Geschäftsgründen, zum Vergnügen oder als Vorbereitung für einen Auslandsurlaub lernen, oder Ihr Vokabular in einer Ihnen bereits vertrauten Sprache erweitern möchten, dieses Wörterbuch ist ein wertvolles Lernmittel, das Sie auf vielfältige Art und Weise benutzen können.

Wenn Sie eine neue Sprache lernen, achten Sie auf Wörter, die in verschiedenen Sprachen ähnlich sind sowie auf falsche Freunde (Wörter, die ähnlich aussehen aber wesentlich andere Bedeutungen haben). Sie können ebenfalls feststellen, wie die Sprachen einander beeinflusst haben. Englisch hat zum Beispiel viele Ausdrücke für Nahrungsmittel aus anderen europäischen Sprachen übernommen und andererseits viele Begriffe aus der Technik und Popkultur ausgeführt.

### Praktische Übungen

• Versuchen Sie sich zu Hause, am Arbeits- oder Studienplatz den Inhalt der Seiten einzuprägen, die Ihre Umgebung behandeln. Schließen Sie dann das Buch und prüfen Sie, wie viele Gegenstände Sie in den anderen Sprachen sagen können.
• Schreiben Sie eine Geschichte, einen Brief oder Dialog und benutzen Sie dabei möglichst viele Ausdrücke von einer bestimmten Seite des Wörterbuchs. Dies ist eine gute Methode, sich das Vokabular und die Schreibweise einzuprägen. Sie können mit kurzen Sätzen von zwei bis drei Worten anfangen und dann nach und nach längere Texte schreiben.
• Wenn Sie ein visuelles Gedächtnis haben, können Sie Gegenstände aus dem Buch abzeichnen oder abpausen. Schließen Sie dann das Buch und schreiben Sie die passenden Wörter unter die Bilder.
• Wenn Sie mehr Sicherheit haben, können Sie Wörter aus einem der Fremdsprachenregister aussuchen und deren Bedeutung aufschreiben, bevor Sie auf der entsprechenden Seite nachsehen.

# Kostenlose Audio-App

Die Audio-App enthält alle Begriffe und Redewendungen aus dem Buch, gesprochen von deutschen und englischen Muttersprachlern.
Das Anhören der Wörter erleichtert das Lernen von wichtigen Vokabeln und das Verbessern Ihrer eigenen Aussprache.

# So funktioniert die Audio-App

• Laden Sie sich die kostenlose App auf Ihr Smartphone oder Tablet vom App-Store Ihres Betriebssystems.
• Öffnen Sie die App und schalten Sie sich die Inhalte Ihres Visuellen Wörterbuchs frei.
• Laden Sie sich die Audio-Daten für Ihr Buch herunter.
• Geben Sie eine Seitenzahl ein, scrollen Sie anschließend in der Wörterliste nach oben oder unten, um einen Begriff oder eine Redewendung zu finden.
• Tippen Sie auf ein Wort, um es sich anzuhören.
• Wischen Sie nach links oder rechts, um sich die vorige oder nächste Seite anzusehen.

# about the dictionary

The use of pictures is proven to aid understanding and the retention of information. Working on this principle, this highly illustrated bilingual dictionary presents a large range of useful current vocabulary in two European languages.

The dictionary is divided thematically and covers most aspects of the everyday world in detail, from the restaurant to the gym, the home to the workplace, outer space to the animal kingdom. You will also find additional words and phrases for conversational use and for extending your vocabulary.

This is an essential reference tool for anyone interested in languages—practical, stimulating, and easy to use.

## A few things to note

The two languages are always presented in the same order—German and English.

In German, nouns are given with their definite articles reflecting the gender (masculine, feminine or neuter) and number (singular or plural), for example:

**der Samen**    **die Mandeln**
seed           almonds

Verbs are indicated by a (v) after the English, for example:

**ernten** • harvest (v)

Each language also has its own index at the back of the book. Here you can look up a word in either of the two languages and be referred to the page number(s) where it appears. The gender is shown using the following abbreviations:

m = masculine
f = feminine
n = neuter

# how to use this book

Whether you are learning a new language for business, pleasure, or in preparation for an overseas vacation, or are hoping to extend your vocabulary in an already familiar language, this dictionary is a valuable learning tool that you can use in a number of different ways.

When learning a new language, look for cognates (words that are alike in different languages) and "false friends" (words that look alike but carry significantly different meanings). You can also see where the languages have influenced each other. For example, English has imported many terms for food from other European languages but, in turn, exported terms used in technology and popular culture.

## Practical learning activities

• As you move around your home, workplace, or school, try looking at the pages which cover that setting. You could then close the book, look around you, and see how many of the objects and features you can name.
• Challenge yourself to write a story, letter, or dialogue using as many of the terms on a particular page as possible. This will help you retain the vocabulary and remember the spelling. If you want to build up to writing a longer text, start with sentences incorporating 2–3 words.
• If you have a very visual memory, try drawing or tracing items from the book onto a piece of paper, then closing the book and filling in the words below the picture.
• Once you are more confident, pick out words in a foreign-language index and see if you know what they mean before turning to the relevant page to check if you were right.

# free audio app

The audio app contains all the words and phrases in the book, spoken by native speakers in both German and English, making it easier to learn important vocabulary and improve your pronunciation.

**FREE AUDIO APP**

# how to use the audio app

• Download the free app on your smartphone or tablet from your chosen app store.
• Open the app and unlock your *Visual Dictionary* in the Library.
• Download the audio files for your book.
• Enter a page number, then scroll up and down through the list to find a word or phrase.
• Tap a word to hear it.
• Swipe left or right to view the previous or next page.

**die Menschen**
people

# der Körper • body

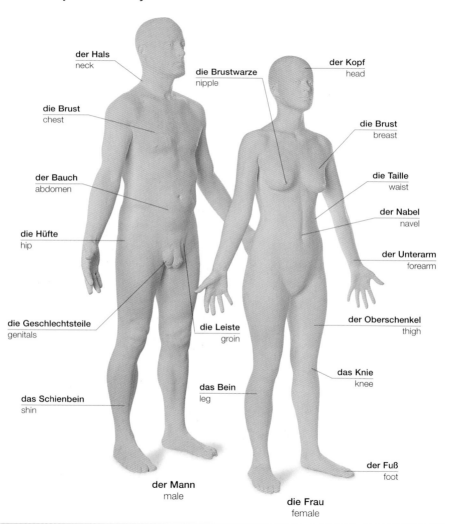

**der Hals**
neck

**die Brustwarze**
nipple

**der Kopf**
head

**die Brust**
chest

**die Brust**
breast

**der Bauch**
abdomen

**die Taille**
waist

**die Hüfte**
hip

**der Nabel**
navel

**der Unterarm**
forearm

**die Geschlechtsteile**
genitals

**die Leiste**
groin

**der Oberschenkel**
thigh

**das Knie**
knee

**das Schienbein**
shin

**das Bein**
leg

**der Fuß**
foot

**der Mann**
male

**die Frau**
female

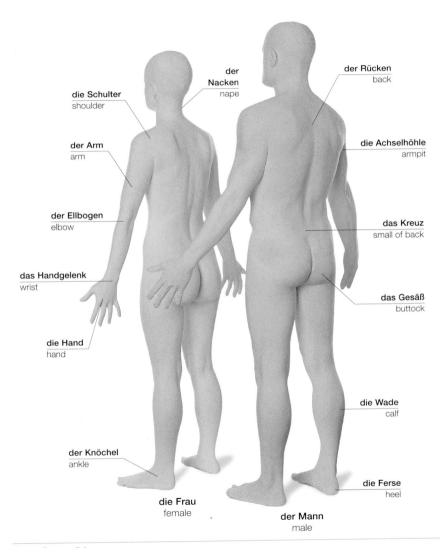

**der Nacken**
nape

**die Schulter**
shoulder

**der Rücken**
back

**der Arm**
arm

**die Achselhöhle**
armpit

**der Ellbogen**
elbow

**das Kreuz**
small of back

**das Handgelenk**
wrist

**das Gesäß**
buttock

**die Hand**
hand

**die Wade**
calf

**der Knöchel**
ankle

**die Ferse**
heel

**die Frau**
female

**der Mann**
male

# das Gesicht • face

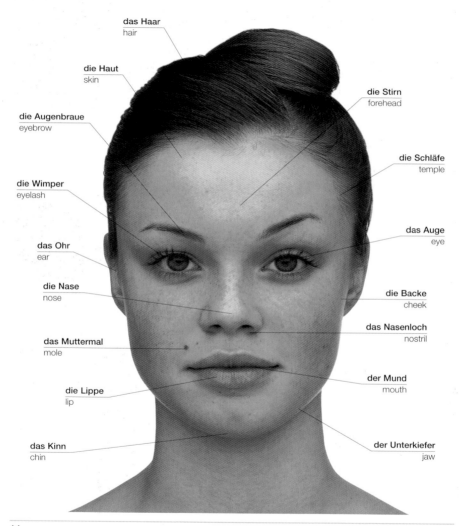

**das Haar**
hair

**die Haut**
skin

**die Augenbraue**
eyebrow

**die Wimper**
eyelash

**das Ohr**
ear

**die Nase**
nose

**das Muttermal**
mole

**die Lippe**
lip

**das Kinn**
chin

**die Stirn**
forehead

**die Schläfe**
temple

**das Auge**
eye

**die Backe**
cheek

**das Nasenloch**
nostril

**der Mund**
mouth

**der Unterkiefer**
jaw

**die Falte**
wrinkle

**die Sommersprosse**
freckle

**die Pore**
pore

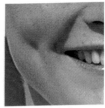

**das Grübchen**
dimple

## die Hand • hand

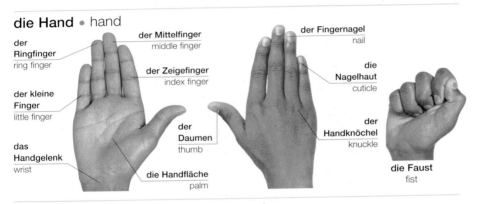

**der Ringfinger**
ring finger

**der Mittelfinger**
middle finger

**der Zeigefinger**
index finger

**der kleine Finger**
little finger

**der Fingernagel**
nail

**die Nagelhaut**
cuticle

**der Handknöchel**
knuckle

**das Handgelenk**
wrist

**der Daumen**
thumb

**die Handfläche**
palm

**die Faust**
fist

## der Fuß • foot

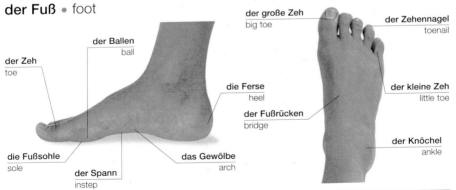

**der Ballen**
ball

**der große Zeh**
big toe

**der Zehennagel**
toenail

**der Zeh**
toe

**die Ferse**
heel

**der Fußrücken**
bridge

**der kleine Zeh**
little toe

**die Fußsohle**
sole

**der Spann**
instep

**das Gewölbe**
arch

**der Knöchel**
ankle

# die Muskeln • muscles

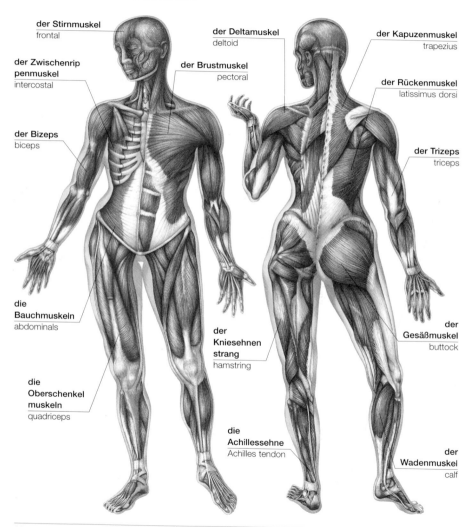

**der Stirnmuskel**
frontal

**der Zwischenrip
penmuskel**
intercostal

**der Bizeps**
biceps

**die
Bauchmuskeln**
abdominals

**die
Oberschenkel
muskeln**
quadriceps

**der Deltamuskel**
deltoid

**der Brustmuskel**
pectoral

**der
Kniesehnen
strang**
hamstring

**die
Achillessehne**
Achilles tendon

**der Kapuzenmuskel**
trapezius

**der Rückenmuskel**
latissimus dorsi

**der Trizeps**
triceps

**der
Gesäßmuskel**
buttock

**der
Wadenmuskel**
calf

# das Skelett • skeleton

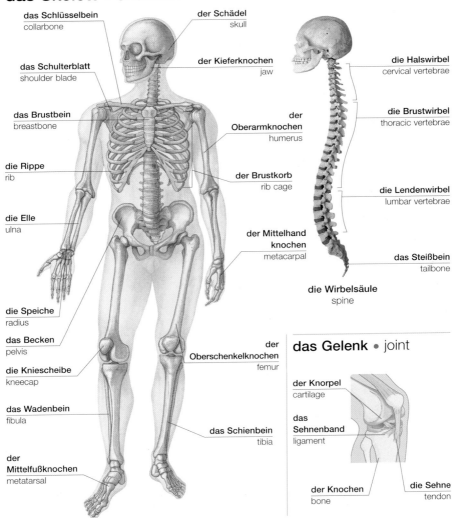

das Schlüsselbein
collarbone

der Schädel
skull

das Schulterblatt
shoulder blade

der Kieferknochen
jaw

die Halswirbel
cervical vertebrae

das Brustbein
breastbone

der
Oberarmknochen
humerus

die Brustwirbel
thoracic vertebrae

die Rippe
rib

der Brustkorb
rib cage

die Elle
ulna

die Lendenwirbel
lumbar vertebrae

der Mittelhand
knochen
metacarpal

die Speiche
radius

das Steißbein
tailbone

das Becken
pelvis

die Wirbelsäule
spine

der
Oberschenkelknochen
femur

die Kniescheibe
kneecap

## das Gelenk • joint

das Wadenbein
fibula

der Knorpel
cartilage

das Schienbein
tibia

das
Sehnenband
ligament

der
Mittelfußknochen
metatarsal

der Knochen
bone

die Sehne
tendon

# die inneren Organe • internal organs

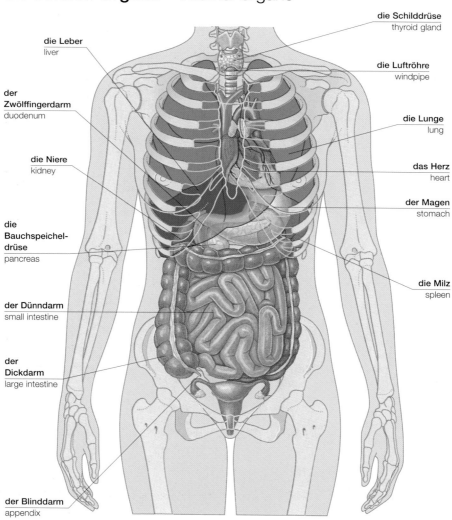

**die Schilddrüse**
thyroid gland

**die Leber**
liver

**die Luftröhre**
windpipe

**der Zwölffingerdarm**
duodenum

**die Lunge**
lung

**die Niere**
kidney

**das Herz**
heart

**der Magen**
stomach

**die Bauchspeicheldrüse**
pancreas

**die Milz**
spleen

**der Dünndarm**
small intestine

**der Dickdarm**
large intestine

**der Blinddarm**
appendix

# der Kopf • head

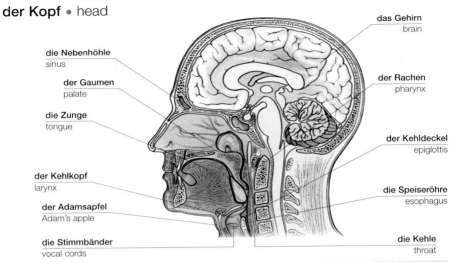

die Nebenhöhle
sinus

der Gaumen
palate

die Zunge
tongue

der Kehlkopf
larynx

der Adamsapfel
Adam's apple

die Stimmbänder
vocal cords

das Gehirn
brain

der Rachen
pharynx

der Kehldeckel
epiglottis

die Speiseröhre
esophagus

die Kehle
throat

# die Körpersysteme • body systems

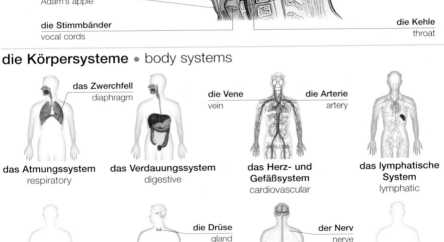

das Zwerchfell
diaphragm

**das Atmungssystem**
respiratory

**das Verdauungssystem**
digestive

die Vene
vein

die Arterie
artery

**das Herz- und
Gefäßsystem**
cardiovascular

**das lymphatische
System**
lymphatic

die Drüse
gland

der Nerv
nerve

**das Harnsystem**
urinary

**das endokrine System**
endocrine

**das Nervensystem**
nervous

**das Fortpflanzungssystem**
reproductive

# die Fortpflanzungsorgane • reproductive organs

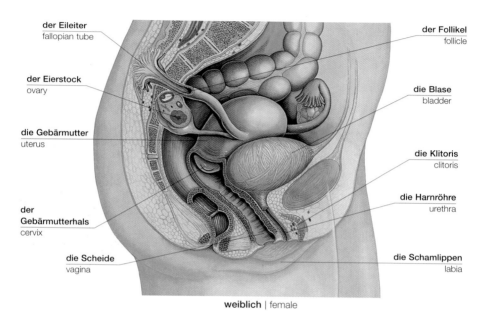

der Eileiter
fallopian tube

der Eierstock
ovary

die Gebärmutter
uterus

der
Gebärmutterhals
cervix

die Scheide
vagina

der Follikel
follicle

die Blase
bladder

die Klitoris
clitoris

die Harnröhre
urethra

die Schamlippen
labia

**weiblich** | female

## die Fortpflanzung • reproduction

das Spermium
sperm

das Ei
egg

**die Befruchtung** | fertilization

**Vokabular** • vocabulary

| | | |
|---|---|---|
| **steril**<br>infertile | **impotent**<br>impotent | **die Menstruation**<br>menstruation |
| **fruchtbar**<br>fertile | **empfangen**<br>conceive | **der Geschlechtsverkehr**<br>intercourse |
| **das Hormon**<br>hormone | **der Eisprung**<br>ovulation | **die Geschlechtskrankheit**<br>sexually transmitted disease |

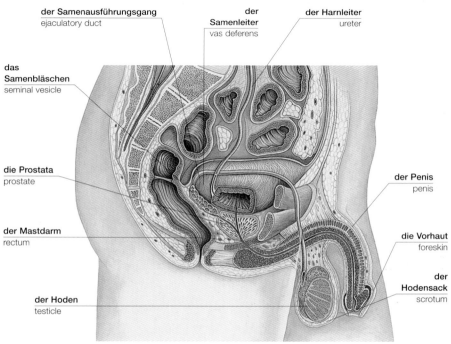

der Samenausführungsgang
ejaculatory duct

der
Samenleiter
vas deferens

der Harnleiter
ureter

das
Samenbläschen
seminal vesicle

die Prostata
prostate

der Penis
penis

der Mastdarm
rectum

die Vorhaut
foreskin

der
Hodensack
scrotum

der Hoden
testicle

**männlich** | male

# die Empfängnisverhütung • contraception

**das Pessar**
cervical cap

**das Diaphragma**
diaphragm

**das Kondom**
condom

**die Spirale**
IUD

**die Pille**
pill

# die Familie • family

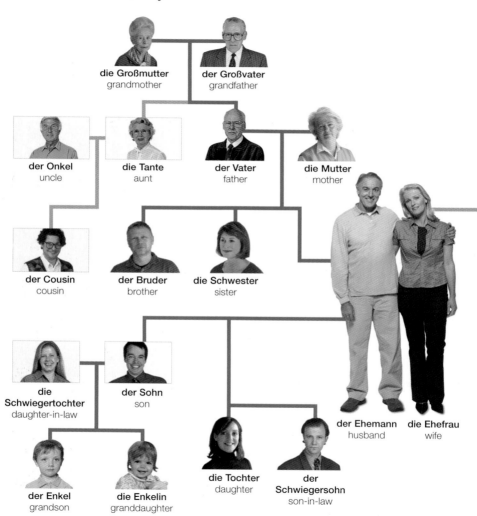

**die Großmutter**
grandmother

**der Großvater**
grandfather

**der Onkel**
uncle

**die Tante**
aunt

**der Vater**
father

**die Mutter**
mother

**der Cousin**
cousin

**der Bruder**
brother

**die Schwester**
sister

**die Schwiegertochter**
daughter-in-law

**der Sohn**
son

**der Ehemann**
husband

**die Ehefrau**
wife

**der Enkel**
grandson

**die Enkelin**
granddaughter

**die Tochter**
daughter

**der Schwiegersohn**
son-in-law

## Vokabular • vocabulary

| | | | | | |
|---|---|---|---|---|---|
| **die Großeltern** grandparents | **die Verwandten** relatives | **die Enkelkinder** grandchildren | **die Stiefmutter** stepmother | **die Stieftochter** stepdaughter | **die Generation** generation |
| **die Eltern** parents | **die Kinder** children | **der Stiefvater** stepfather | **der Stiefsohn** stepson | **der Partner/die Partnerin** partner | **die Zwillinge** twins |

## die Stadien • stages

**die Schwiegermutter** mother-in-law

**der Schwiegervater** father-in-law

**der Schwager** brother-in-law

**die Schwägerin** sister-in-law

**die Nichte** niece

**der Neffe** nephew

Frau
Mrs.

## die Anreden • titles

Herr
Mr.

Fräulein
Miss/Ms.

**das Baby** baby

**das Kind** child

**der Junge** boy

**das Mädchen** girl

**die Jugendliche** teenager

**der Erwachsene** adult

**der Mann** man

**die Frau** woman

# die Beziehungen • relationships

die Assistentin
assistant

der Chef
manager

die Geschäftspartnerin
business partner

der Arbeitnehmer
employee

die Arbeitgeberin
employer

der Kollege
colleague

**das Büro** | office

**die Nachbarin**
neighbor

**der Freund**
friend

**der Bekannte**
acquaintance

**der Brieffreund**
pen pal

der Freund
boyfriend

die Freundin
girlfriend

**das Paar** | couple

der Verlobte
fiancé

die Verlobte
fiancée

**die Verlobten** | engaged couple

# die Gefühle • emotions

das Lächeln
smile

**glücklich**
happy

**traurig**
sad

**begeistert**
excited

**gelangweilt**
bored

**überrascht**
surprised

**erschrocken**
scared

das
**Stirnrunzeln**
frown

**verärgert**
angry

**verwirrt**
confused

**besorgt**
worried

**nervös**
nervous

**stolz**
proud

**selbstsicher**
confident

**verlegen**
embarrassed

**schüchtern**
shy

| **Vokabular** • vocabulary | | | |
|---|---|---|---|
| **aufgebracht** upset | **schreien** shout (v) | **lachen** laugh (v) | **seufzen** sigh (v) |
| **schockiert** shocked | **gähnen** yawn (v) | **weinen** cry (v) | **in Ohnmacht fallen** faint (v) |

# die Ereignisse des Lebens • life events

**geboren werden**
be born (v)

**zur Schule kommen**
start school (v)

**sich anfreunden**
make friends (v)

**graduieren**
graduate (v)

**eine Stelle bekommen**
get a job (v)

**sich verlieben**
fall in love (v)

**heiraten**
get married (v)

**ein Baby bekommen**
have a baby (v)

**die Hochzeit** | wedding

**die Scheidung**
divorce

**das Begräbnis**
funeral

## vokabular • vocabulary

**die Taufe**
christening

**die Bar-Mizwa**
bar mitzvah

**der Hochzeitstag**
anniversary

**in den Ruhestand treten**
retire (v)

**sein Testament machen**
make a will (v)

**emigrieren**
emigrate (v)

**sterben**
die (v)

**die Hochzeitsfeier**
wedding reception

**die Hochzeitsreise**
honeymoon

**die Geburtsurkunde**
birth certificate

# die Feste • celebrations

die
**Geburtstagsfeier**
birthday party

**die Karte**
card

**der Geburtstag**
birthday

**das Geschenk**
present

**das Weihnachten**
Christmas

# die Feiern •
festivals

**das Passah**
Passover

**das Neujahr**
New Year

**der Karneval**
carnival

**der Umzug**
procession

**der Ramadan**
Ramadan

**das Band**
ribbon

**das Erntedankfest**
Thanksgiving

**das Ostern**
Easter

**das Halloween**
Halloween

**das Diwali**
Diwali

**die äußere Erscheinung**
appearance

# die Kinderkleidung • children's clothing

## das Baby • baby

**der Schneeanzug**
snowsuit

**das Hemdchen**
bodysuit

**der Druckknopf**
snap

**der Strampelanzug**
onesie

**der Schlafanzug**
sleeper

**der Spielanzug**
romper

**das Lätzchen**
bib

**die Babyhandschuhe**
mittens

**die Babyschuhe**
booties

**die Stoffwindel**
cloth diaper

**die Wegwerfwindel**
disposable diaper

**das Gummihöschen**
plastic pants

## das Kleinkind • toddler

**der Sonnenhut**
sun hat

**die Schürze**
apron

**die Latzhose**
overalls

**die Shorts**
shorts

**das T-Shirt**
T-shirt

**der Rock**
skirt

# das Kind • child

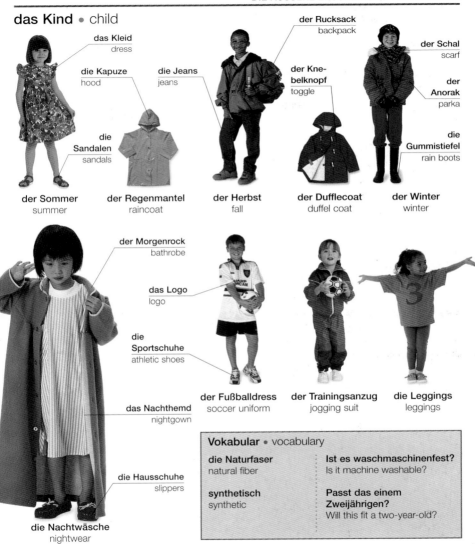

das Kleid
dress

die Kapuze
hood

die Jeans
jeans

die Sandalen
sandals

der Sommer
summer

der Regenmantel
raincoat

der Rucksack
backpack

der Knebelknopf
toggle

der Herbst
fall

der Dufflecoat
duffel coat

der Schal
scarf

der Anorak
parka

die Gummistiefel
rain boots

der Winter
winter

der Morgenrock
bathrobe

das Logo
logo

die Sportschuhe
athletic shoes

das Nachthemd
nightgown

die Hausschuhe
slippers

die Nachtwäsche
nightwear

der Fußballdress
soccer uniform

der Trainingsanzug
jogging suit

die Leggings
leggings

## Vokabular • vocabulary

die Naturfaser
natural fiber

synthetisch
synthetic

Ist es waschmaschinenfest?
Is it machine washable?

Passt das einem Zweijährigen?
Will this fit a two-year-old?

# die Herrenkleidung • men's clothing

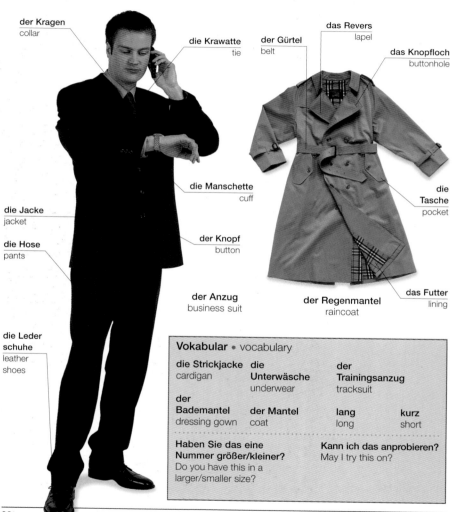

der Kragen
collar

die Krawatte
tie

der Gürtel
belt

das Revers
lapel

das Knopfloch
buttonhole

die Manschette
cuff

die
Tasche
pocket

die Jacke
jacket

die Hose
pants

der Knopf
button

der Anzug
business suit

der Regenmantel
raincoat

das Futter
lining

die Leder
schuhe
leather
shoes

---

**Vokabular • vocabulary**

| | | |
|---|---|---|
| die Strickjacke | die | der |
| cardigan | Unterwäsche | Trainingsanzug |
| | underwear | tracksuit |
| der | | |
| Bademantel | der Mantel | lang | kurz |
| dressing gown | coat | long | short |

Haben Sie das eine
Nummer größer/kleiner?
Do you have this in a
larger/smaller size?

Kann ich das anprobieren?
May I try this on?

**der Blazer**
blazer

**das Sportjackett**
sport coat

**die Weste**
vest

der V-Ausschnitt
V-neck

**der runde Ausschnitt**
crew neck

**das T-Shirt**
T-shirt

**der Anorak**
parka

**das Sweatshirt**
sweatshirt

**das Hemd**
shirt

**die Jeans**
jeans

**der Pullover**
sweater

**der Schlafanzug**
pajamas

**das Unterhemd**
undershirt

**die Freizeitkleidung**
casual wear

**die Shorts**
shorts

**der Slip**
briefs

**die Boxershorts**
boxer shorts

**die Socken**
socks

# die Damenkleidung • women's clothing

die Jacke
jacket

die Naht
seam

trägerlos
strapless

ärmellos
sleeveless

der Ärmel
sleeve

knöchellang
ankle length

das Abendkleid
evening dress

das Kleid
dress

der Rock
skirt

die Bluse
blouse

der Saum
hem

knielang
knee-length

die Hose
pants

die Schuhe
shoes

formell
formal

leger
casual

# die Unterwäsche • lingerie

# die Hochzeit • wedding

**der Morgenmantel**
robe

**der Unterrock**
slip

**der Träger**
strap

**das Mieder**
camisole

**das Bustier**
bustier

**der Strumpfhalter**
garter straps

**der Strumpf**
stocking

**die Strumpfhose**
panty hose

**der Büstenhalter**
bra

**der Slip**
panties

**das Nachthemd**
nightgown

**die Spitze**
lace

**der Schleier**
veil

**das Bukett**
bouquet

**die Schleppe**
train

**das Hochzeitskleid**
wedding dress

## Vokabular • vocabulary

| | |
|---|---|
| **das Korsett** corset | **gut geschnitten** tailored |
| **rückenfrei** halter neck | **das Strumpfband** garter |
| **der Rockbund** waistband | **der Sport-BH** sports bra |
| **das Schulter polster** shoulder pad | **mit Formbügeln** underwire |

# die Accessoires • accessories

**die
Gürtelschnalle**
buckle

**der Griff**
handle

**die Mütze**
cap

**der Hut**
hat

**das Halstuch**
scarf

**der Gürtel**
belt

**die Spitze**
tip

**das Taschentuch**
handkerchief

**die Fliege**
bow tie

**die
Krawattennadel**
tiepin

**die Handschuhe**
gloves

**der Regenschirm**
umbrella

# der Schmuck • jewelry

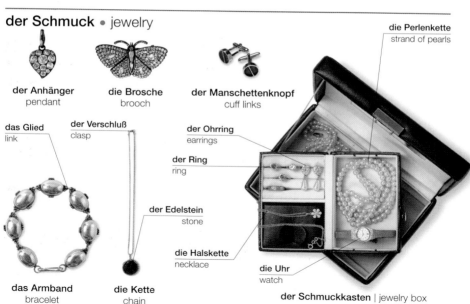

**die Perlenkette**
strand of pearls

**der Anhänger**
pendant

**die Brosche**
brooch

**der Manschettenknopf**
cuff links

**das Glied**
link

**der Verschluß**
clasp

**der Ohrring**
earrings

**der Ring**
ring

**der Edelstein**
stone

**die Halskette**
necklace

**die Uhr**
watch

**das Armband**
bracelet

**die Kette**
chain

**der Schmuckkasten | jewelry box**

# die Taschen • bags

**die Brieftasche**
wallet

**das Portemonnaie**
change purse

der Verschluss
clasp

**die Umhängetasche**
shoulder bag

die Griffe
handles

der Schulterriemen
shoulder strap

**die Reisetasche**
duffel bag

**die Aktentasche**
briefcase

**die Handtasche**
handbag

**der Rucksack**
backpack

# die Schuhe • shoes

der Schnürsenkel
lace

die Zunge
tongue

die Öse
eyelet

die Sohle
sole

**der Schnürschuh**
lace-up

der Absatz
heel

**der Wanderschuh**
hiking boot

**der Sportschuh**
sneaker

**der Stiefel**
boot

**die Strandsandale**
flip-flop

**der Herrenhalbschuh**
dress shoe

**der Schuh mit hohem Absatz**
high-heeled shoe

**der Keilschuh**
wedge

**die Sandale**
sandal

**der Slipper**
slip-on

**der Pumps**
pump

# das Haar • hair

**der Kamm**
comb

**kämmen**
comb (v)

**die Haarbürste**
brush

**bürsten** | brush (v)

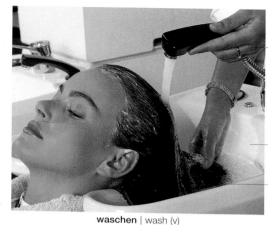

**die Friseurin**
hairdresser

**das Waschbecken**
sink

**die Kundin**
client

**waschen** | wash (v)

**ausspülen**
rinse (v)

**der Frisierumhang**
robe

**schneiden**
cut (v)

**föhnen**
blow-dry (v)

**legen**
set (v)

# die Frisierartikel • accessories

**der Föhn**
blow-dryer

**das Shampoo**
shampoo

**die Haarspülung**
conditioner

**das Haargel**
gel

**das Haarspray**
hairspray

**der Lockenstab**
curling iron

**die Schere**
scissors

**der Haarreif**
headband

**der Haarglätter**
hair straightener

**die Haarklammer**
bobby pins

# die Frisuren • styles

**der Pferdeschwanz**
ponytail

**der Zopf**
braid

**die Hochfrisur**
French twist

**der Haarknoten**
bun

**die Schwänzchen**
pigtails

**der Bubikopf**
bob

**der Kurzhaarschnitt**
crop

**lockig**
curly

**die Dauerwelle**
perm

**glatt**
straight

**die Wurzeln**
roots

**die Strähnen**
highlights

**kahl**
bald

**die Perücke**
wig

| **Vokabular** • vocabulary | |
|---|---|
| **das Haarband** hairband | **fettig** greasy |
| **nachschneiden** trim (v) | **trocken** dry |
| **der Herrenfriseur** barber | **normal** normal |
| **die Schuppen** dandruff | **die Kopfhaut** scalp |
| **der Haarspliss** split ends | **glätten** straighten (v) |

# die Haarfarben • colors

**blond**
blonde

**brünett**
brunette

**rotbraun**
auburn

**rot**
red

**schwarz**
black

**grau**
gray

**weiß**
white

**gefärbt**
dyed

# die Schönheit • beauty

**das Haarfärbemittel**
hair dye

**der Lidschatten**
eye shadow

**die Wimperntusche**
mascara

**der Eyeliner**
eyeliner

**das Puderrouge**
blush

**die Grundierung**
foundation

**der Lippenstift**
lipstick

## das Make-up • makeup

**der Augenbrauenstift**
eyebrow pencil

**das Brauenbürstchen**
eyebrow brush

**die Pinzette**
tweezers

**das Lipgloss**
lip gloss

**der Lippenpinsel**
lip brush

**der Lippenkonturenstift**
lip liner

**der Puderpinsel**
brush

**der Korrekturstift**
concealer

**der Spiegel**
mirror

**der Gesichtspuder**
face powder

**die Puderquaste**
powder puff

**die Puderdose** | compact

# die Schönheitsbehandlungen •
beauty treatments

**die Gesichtsmaske**
face mask

**die Sonnenbank**
sunbed

**die Gesichtsbehandlung**
facial

**Peeling machen**
exfoliate (v)

**die Enthaarung**
wax

**die Pediküre**
pedicure

# die Maniküre • manicure

**der Nagellackentferner**
nail polish remover

**die Nagelfeile**
nail file

**der Nagellack**
nail polish

**die Nagelschere**
nail scissors

**der Nagelknipser**
nail clippers

# die Toilettenartikel • toiletries

**der Reiniger**
cleanser

**das Gesichts-wasser**
toner

**die Feuchtig-keitscreme**
moisturizer

**die Selbst-bräunungscreme**
self-tanning lotion

**das Parfum**
perfume

**das Eau de Toilette**
eau de toilette

---

**Vokabular** • vocabulary

| | | |
|---|---|---|
| **die Sonnenbräune** tan | **empfindlich** sensitive | **hell** fair |
| **die Tätowierung** tattoo | **der Farbton** shade | **dunkel** dark |
| **die Wattebällchen** cotton balls | **Antifalten-** antiwrinkle | **trocken** dry |
| **hypoallergen** hypoallergenic | **der Teint** complexion | **fettig** oily |

---

**die Gesundheit**
health

# die Krankheit • illness

das Fieber | fever

die Kopfschmerzen
headache

das Nasenbluten
nosebleed

der Husten
cough

das Niesen
sneeze

die Erkältung
cold

die Grippe
flu

der Inhalations apparat
inhaler

das Asthma
asthma

die Krämpfe
cramps

die Übelkeit
nausea

die Windpocken
chicken pox

der Hautausschlag
rash

## Vokabular • vocabulary

| | | | | | |
|---|---|---|---|---|---|
| der Herzinfarkt heart attack | die Allergie allergy | das Ekzem eczema | die Verkühlung chill | die Epilepsie epilepsy | der Durchfall diarrhea |
| der Blutdruck blood pressure | der Mumps mumps | der Virus virus | die Migräne migraine | sich übergeben vomit (v) | die Masern measles |
| der Schlaganfall stroke | die Zucker krankheit diabetes | die Infektion infection | die Magenschmerzen stomachache | in Ohnmacht fallen faint (v) | der Heuschnupfen hay fever |

# der Arzt • doctor
## die Konsultation • consultation

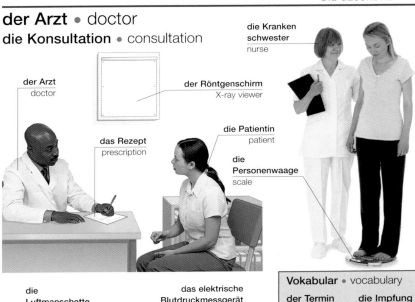

die Kranken schwester
nurse

der Arzt
doctor

der Röntgenschirm
X-ray viewer

das Rezept
prescription

die Patientin
patient

die Personenwaage
scale

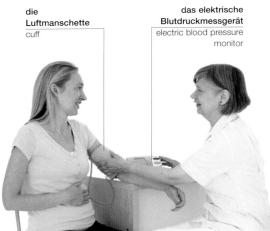

die Luftmanschette
cuff

das elektrische Blutdruckmessgerät
electric blood pressure monitor

## Vokabular • vocabulary

| | |
|---|---|
| **der Termin** appointment | **die Impfung** vaccination |
| **das Sprechzimmer** doctor's office | **die Untersuchung** medical examination |
| **der Warteraum** waiting room | **das Thermometer** thermometer |

**Ich muss mit einem Arzt sprechen.**
I need to see a doctor.

**Es tut hier weh.**
It hurts here.

# die Verletzung • injury

die Schlinge
sling

die
Halskrawatte
neck brace

**die Verstauchung** | sprain

**die Fraktur**
fracture

**das Schleudertrauma**
whiplash

**der Schnitt**
cut

**die Abschürfung**
graze

**der blaue Fleck**
bruise

**der Splitter**
splinter

**der Sonnenbrand**
sunburn

**die Brandwunde**
burn

**der Biss**
bite

**der Stich**
sting

## Vokabular • vocabulary

| | | | |
|---|---|---|---|
| **der Unfall**<br>accident | **die Blutung**<br>hemorrhage | **die Kopfverletzung**<br>head injury | **Wird er/sie es gut überstehen?**<br>Will he/she be all right? |
| **der Notfall**<br>emergency | **die Blase**<br>blister | **die Vergiftung**<br>poisoning | **Rufen Sie bitte einen Krankenwagen.**<br>Please call an ambulance. |
| **die Wunde**<br>wound | **der elektrische Schlag**<br>electric shock | **die Gehirnerschütterung**<br>concussion | **Wo haben Sie Schmerzen?**<br>Where does it hurt? |

# die erste Hilfe • first aid

die Salbe
ointment

das Pflaster
adhesive bandage

die Sicherheitsnadel
safety pin

die Bandage
bandage

die Schmerz tabletten
painkillers

das Desinfektionstuch
antiseptic wipe

die Pinzette
tweezers

die Schere
scissors

das Antiseptikum
antiseptic

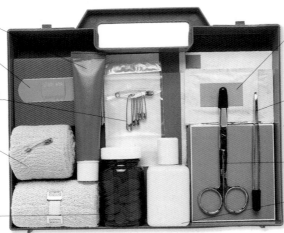

**der Erste-Hilfe-Kasten** | first-aid kit

die Gaze
gauze

**der Verband**
dressing

**die Schiene** | splint

das Leukoplast
adhesive tape

**die Wiederbelebung**
resuscitation

| **Vokabular** • vocabulary | | | |
|---|---|---|---|
| der Schock shock | der Puls pulse | ersticken choke (v) | **Können Sie mir helfen?** Can you help? |
| bewusstlos unconscious | die Atmung breathing | steril sterile | **Beherrschen Sie die Erste Hilfe?** Do you know first aid? |

# das Krankenhaus • hospital

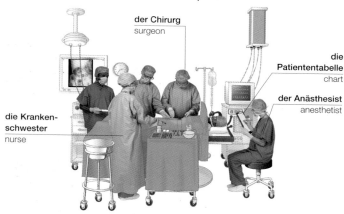

**der Chirurg**
surgeon

**die Kranken-
schwester**
nurse

**der Operationssaal**
operating room

die
**Patiententabelle**
chart

**der Anästhesist**
anesthetist

**die Blutuntersuchung**
blood test

**die Spritze**
injection

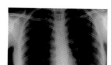

**die Röntgenaufnahme**
X-ray

die
**fahrbare Liege**
gurney

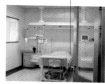

**die Notaufnahme**
emergency room

**der Rufknopf**
call button

**die
Krankenhausstation**
ward

**der Rollstuhl**
wheelchair

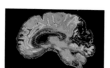

**der CT-Scan**
scan

---

**Vokabular** • vocabulary

| | | | | |
|---|---|---|---|---|
| **die Operation**<br>operation | **entlassen**<br>discharged | **die Besuchszeiten**<br>visiting hours | **die Entbindungsstation**<br>maternity ward | **die Intensivstation**<br>intensive care unit |
| **aufgenommen**<br>admitted | **die Klinik**<br>clinic | **die Kinderstation**<br>children's ward | **das Privatzimmer**<br>private room | **der ambulante Patient**<br>outpatient |

# die Abteilungen • departments

**die HNO-Abteilung**
ENT

**die Kardiologie**
cardiology

**die Orthopädie**
orthopedics

**die Gynäkologie**
gynecology

**die Physiotherapie**
physiotherapy

**die Dermatologie**
dermatology

**die Pädiatrie**
pediatrics

**die Radiologie**
radiology

**die Chirurgie**
surgery

**die Entbindungsstation**
maternity

**die Psychiatrie**
psychiatry

**die Ophthalmologie**
ophthalmology

---

**Vokabular • vocabulary**

| | | | | |
|---|---|---|---|---|
| **die Neurologie** neurology | **die Urologie** urology | **die plastische Chirurgie** plastic surgery | **die Pathologie** pathology | **das Ergebnis** result |
| **die Onkologie** oncology | **die Endokrinologie** endocrinology | **die Überweisung** referral | **die Untersuchung** test | **der Facharzt** specialist |

---

# der Zahnarzt • dentist

## der Zahn • tooth

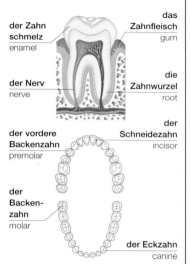

der Zahn
schmelz
enamel

das
**Zahnfleisch**
gum

der Nerv
nerve

die
**Zahnwurzel**
root

der vordere
Backenzahn
premolar

der
**Schneidezahn**
incisor

der
Backen-
zahn
molar

der Eckzahn
canine

---

| **Vokabular** • vocabulary | |
|---|---|
| **der Zahnbelag** plaque | **der Bohrer** drill |
| **die Karies** decay | **die Zahnseide** dental floss |
| **die Zahnfüllung** filling | **die Extraktion** extraction |
| **die Zahnschmerzen** toothache | **die Krone** crown |

## der Check-up • checkup

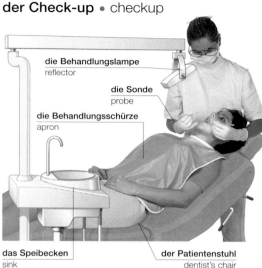

die Behandlungslampe
reflector

die Sonde
probe

die Behandlungsschürze
apron

das Speibecken
sink

der Patientenstuhl
dentist's chair

**mit Zahnseide reinigen**
floss (v)

**bürsten**
brush (v)

**die Zahnspange**
braces

**die Röntgen-aufnahme**
dental X-ray

**das Röntgenbild**
X-ray film

**die Zahnprothese**
dentures

---

# der Augenoptiker • optometrist

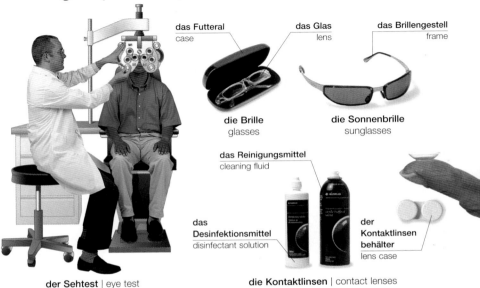

**das Futteral**
case

**das Glas**
lens

**das Brillengestell**
frame

**die Brille**
glasses

**die Sonnenbrille**
sunglasses

**das Reinigungsmittel**
cleaning fluid

**das Desinfektionsmittel**
disinfectant solution

**der Kontaktlinsen behälter**
lens case

**der Sehtest** | eye test

**die Kontaktlinsen** | contact lenses

## das Auge • eye

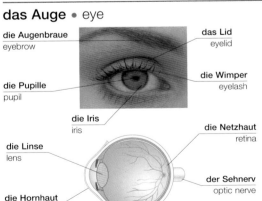

**die Augenbraue**
eyebrow

**das Lid**
eyelid

**die Wimper**
eyelash

**die Pupille**
pupil

**die Iris**
iris

**die Netzhaut**
retina

**die Linse**
lens

**der Sehnerv**
optic nerve

**die Hornhaut**
cornea

| **Vokabular** • vocabulary | |
|---|---|
| **die Sehkraft**<br>vision | **der Astigmatismus**<br>astigmatism |
| **die Dioptrie**<br>diopter | **die Weitsichtigkeit**<br>farsighted |
| **die Träne**<br>tear | **die Kurzsichtigkeit**<br>nearsighted |
| **der graue Star**<br>cataract | **Bifokal-**<br>bifocal |

# die Schwangerschaft • pregnancy

**der Schwangerschaftstest**
pregnancy test

**die Ultraschallaufnahme**
scan

**die Nabelschnur**
umbilical cord

**die Plazenta**
placenta

**der Gebärmutterhals**
cervix

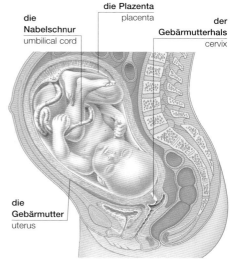

**die Gebärmutter**
uterus

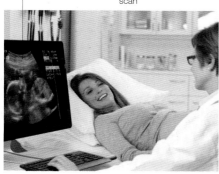

**der Ultraschall** | ultrasound

**der Fetus** | fetus

---

## Vokabular • vocabulary

| | | | | | |
|---|---|---|---|---|---|
| **der Eisprung** ovulation | **vorgeburtlich** prenatal | **das Fruchtwasser** amniotic fluid | **die Erweiterung** dilation | **die Naht** stitches | **die Steißgeburt** breech birth |
| **schwanger** pregnant | **der Embryo** embryo | **die Amniozentese** amniocentesis | **der Kaiserschnitt** cesarean section | **die Geburt** birth | **vorzeitig** premature |
| **die Empfängnis** conception | **die Gebärmutter** womb | **das Fruchtwasser geht ab** break water (v) | **die Periduralanästhesie** epidural | **die Entbindung** delivery | **der Gynäkologe** gynecologist |
| **schwanger** expecting | **das Trimester** trimester | **die Wehe** contraction | **der Dammschnitt** episiotomy | **die Fehlgeburt** miscarriage | **der Geburtshelfer** obstetrician |

# die Geburt • childbirth

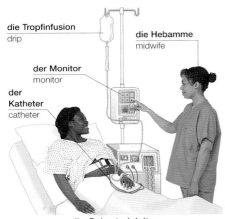

die Tropfinfusion
drip

die Hebamme
midwife

der Monitor
monitor

der Katheter
catheter

**die Geburt einleiten**
induce labor (v)

**der Brutkasten** | incubator

**das Geburtsgewicht**
birth weight

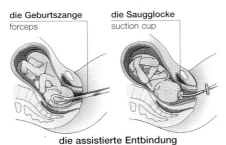

die Geburtszange
forceps

die Saugglocke
suction cup

**die assistierte Entbindung**
assisted delivery

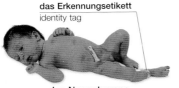

das Erkennungsetikett
identity tag

**das Neugeborene**
newborn baby

## das Stillen • nursing

**die Brustpumpe**
breast pump

**der Stillbüstenhalter**
nursing bra

**stillen**
breastfeed (v)

**die Einlagen**
nursing pads

# die Alternativtherapien • alternative therapy

die Yoga-Haltung
yoga pose

die Matte
mat

**das Yoga** | yoga

**die Massage**
massage

**das Shiatsu**
shiatsu

**die Chiropraktik**
chiropractic

**die Osteopathie**
osteopathy

**die Reflexzonenmassage**
reflexology

**die Meditation**
meditation

**der Berater**
counselor

**die Gruppentherapie**
group therapy

**das Reiki**
reiki

**die Akupunktur**
acupuncture

**das Ayurveda**
ayurveda

**die Hypnotherapie**
hypnotherapy

**die ätherischen Öle**
essential oils

**die Kräuterheilkunde**
herbalism

**die Aromatherapie**
aromatherapy

**die Homöopathie**
homeopathy

**die Akupressur**
acupressure

**die Therapeutin**
therapist

**die Psychotherapie**
psychotherapy

| **Vokabular** • vocabulary | | | |
|---|---|---|---|
| **die Kristalltherapie** crystal healing | **die Naturheilkunde** naturopathy | **der Stress** stress | **das Nahrungsergänzungsmitttel** supplement |
| **die Wasserbe handlung** hydrotherapy | **das Feng Shui** feng shui | **das Heilkraut** herb | **die Entspannung** relaxation |

das Haus
home

# das Haus • house

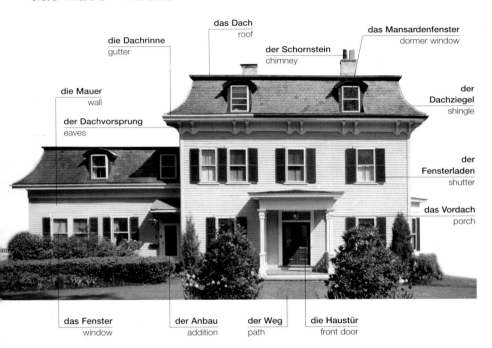

das Dach
roof

die Dachrinne
gutter

der Schornstein
chimney

das Mansardenfenster
dormer window

die Mauer
wall

der Dachvorsprung
eaves

der Dachziegel
shingle

der Fensterladen
shutter

das Vordach
porch

das Fenster
window

der Anbau
addition

der Weg
path

die Haustür
front door

## Vokabular • vocabulary

| | | | | | |
|---|---|---|---|---|---|
| **Einzel(haus)** single-family | **Reihen(haus)** row house | **die Garage** garage | **das Stockwerk** floor | **die Alarmanlage** burglar alarm | **mieten** rent (v) |
| **Doppel(haus)** duplex | **der Bungalow** bungalow | **das Zimmer** room | **der Hof** courtyard | **der Briefkasten** mailbox | **die Miete** rent |
| **das Stadthaus** townhouse | **das Kellergeschoss** basement | **der Dachboden** attic | **die Haustürlampe** porch light | **der Vermieter** landlord | **der Mieter** tenant |

# der Eingang • entrance

das Geländer
hand rail

der Treppen-absatz
landing

das Treppen-geländer
banister

die Treppe
staircase

die Diele
foyer

der Balkon
balcony

der Wohnblock
apartment building

die Sprechanlage
intercom

die Türklingel
doorbell

der Fußabtreter
doormat

der Türklopfer
door knocker

die Türkette
door chain

der Schlüssel
key

das Schloss
lock

der Türriegel
bolt

der Fahrstuhl
elevator

# die Hausanschlüsse · internal systems

der **Flügel**
blade

der **Ventilator**
fan

der **Heizkörper**
radiator

der **Heizofen**
space heater

der **Heizlüfter**
convector heater

# die Elektrizität · electricity

die **Erdung**
ground

der **Pol**
pin

der **Stecker**
plug

neutral
neutral

geladen
live

die **Energiesparlampe**
energy-saving bulb

die **Leitung**
wires

---

**Vokabular** · vocabulary

| | | | | |
|---|---|---|---|---|
| die **Spannung**<br>voltage | die **Sicherung**<br>fuse | die **Steckdose**<br>outlet | der **Gleichstrom**<br>direct current | der **Transformator**<br>transformer |
| das **Ampère**<br>amp | der **Generator**<br>generator | der **Schalter**<br>switch | der **Stromzähler**<br>electric meter | das **Stromnetz**<br>household current |
| der **Strom**<br>power | der **Sicherungskasten**<br>fuse box | der **Wechselstrom**<br>alternating current | der **Stromausfall**<br>power outage | |

---

# die Installation • plumbing

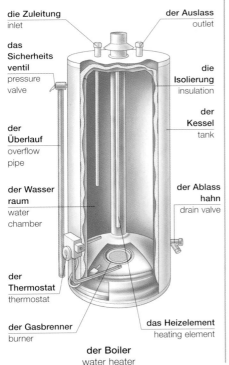

die Zuleitung
inlet

der Auslass
outlet

das
Sicherheits
ventil
pressure
valve

die
Isolierung
insulation

der
Kessel
tank

der
Überlauf
overflow
pipe

der Wasser
raum
water
chamber

der Ablass
hahn
drain valve

der
Thermostat
thermostat

der Gasbrenner
burner

das Heizelement
heating element

der Boiler
water heater

## die Spüle • sink

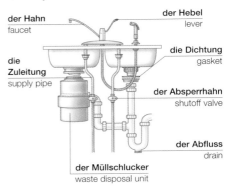

der Hahn
faucet

der Hebel
lever

die Dichtung
gasket

die
Zuleitung
supply pipe

der Absperrhahn
shutoff valve

der Abfluss
drain

der Müllschlucker
waste disposal unit

## die Toilette • toilet

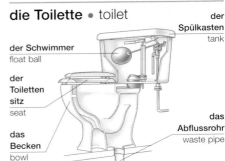

der
Spülkasten
tank

der Schwimmer
float ball

der
Toiletten
sitz
seat

das
Becken
bowl

das
Abflussrohr
waste pipe

# die Abfallentsorgung • waste disposal

die Flasche
bottle

der Deckel
lid

der
Trethebel
pedal

der
Recyclingbehälter
recycling bin

der Abfalleimer
trash can

die
Abfallsortiereinheit
sorting unit

der Bio-Abfall
organic waste

# das Wohnzimmer • living room

**die Wandlampe**
wall light

**der Kamin**
fireplace

**die Decke**
ceiling

**die Vase**
vase

**das Sofakissen**
pillow

**die Lampe**
lamp

**der Couchtisch**
coffee table

**das Sofa**
sofa

**der Fußboden**
floor

der
**Bilderrahmen**
frame

**der Vorhang**
curtain

**die Gardine**
sheer curtain

das **Gemälde**
painting

**die Jalousie**
Venetian blind

**das Rollo**
roller shade

der **Stuck**
molding

der **Sessel**
armchair

das **Bücherregal**
bookshelf

die
**Bettcouch**
sofa bed

der **Teppich**
rug

**das Arbeitszimmer** | study

# das Esszimmer • dining room

**der Pfeffer**
pepper

**das Salz**
salt

**der Tisch**
table

**das Geschirr**
crockery

**das Besteck**
cutlery

**der Stuhl**
chair

**die Lehne**
back

**die Sitzfläche**
seat

**das Bein**
leg

---

## Vokabular • vocabulary

| | | | | | |
|---|---|---|---|---|---|
| **die Tischdecke**<br>tablecloth | **die Gastgeberin**<br>hostess | **die Portion**<br>portion | **den Tisch decken**<br>set the table (v) | **das Frühstück**<br>breakfast | **Könnte ich bitte noch ein bisschen haben?**<br>Can I have some more, please? |
| **das Set**<br>placemat | **der Gast**<br>guest | **hungrig**<br>hungry | **servieren**<br>serve (v) | **das Mittagessen**<br>lunch | **Ich bin satt, danke.**<br>I've had enough, thank you. |
| **das Essen**<br>meal | **der Gastgeber**<br>host | **satt**<br>full | **essen**<br>eat (v) | **das Abendessen**<br>dinner | **Das war lecker.**<br>That was delicious. |

# das Geschirr und das Besteck • crockery and cutlery

**der Becher**
mug

**die Kaffeetasse**
coffee cup

**der Teelöffel**
teaspoon

**die Teetasse**
teacup

**der Teller**
plate

**die Schüssel**
bowl

**die Cafetière**
French press

**die Teekanne**
teapot

**das Kännchen**
pitcher

**der Eierbecher**
egg cup

**das Weinglas**
wine glass

**das Wasserglas**
tumbler

**die Glaswaren**
glassware

**der Serviettenring**
napkin ring

**der Beilagenteller**
side plate

**der Essteller**
dinner plate

**der Suppenteller**
soup bowl

**der Suppenlöffel**
soup spoon

**die Serviette**
napkin

**die Gabel**
fork

**das Gedeck**
place setting

**der Löffel**
spoon

**das Messer**
knife

# die Küche • kitchen

das Küchenregal
shelves

der Spritzschutz
backsplash

der Wasserhahn
faucet

das
Spülbecken
sink

die Schublade
drawer

der Dunstabzug
ventilation hood

das
Glaskeramik
kochfeld
ceramic
stovetop

die
Arbeitsfläche
countertop

der Backofen
oven

der Küchen
schrank
cabinet

## die Küchengeräte • appliances

**die Mikrowelle**
microwave oven

der
**Elektrokessel**
electric kettle

**der Toaster**
toaster

die
**Mixerschüssel**
mixing bowl

das
**Messer**
blade

die
**Küchenmaschine**
food processor

**der Deckel**
lid

**der Mixer**
blender

**die Spülmaschine**
dishwasher

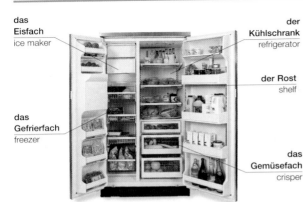

das
**Eisfach**
ice maker

der
**Kühlschrank**
refrigerator

der **Rost**
shelf

das
**Gefrierfach**
freezer

das
**Gemüsefach**
crisper

**der Gefrier-Kühlschrank** | side-by-side refrigerator

---

**Vokabular** • vocabulary

| | |
|---|---|
| **das Kochfeld**<br>stovetop | **einfrieren**<br>freeze (v) |
| **das Abtropfbrett**<br>draining board | **auftauen**<br>defrost (v) |
| **der Brenner**<br>burner | **dämpfen**<br>steam (v) |
| **der Mülleimer**<br>garbage can | **anbraten**<br>sauté (v) |

---

# das Kochen • cooking

**schälen**
peel (v)

**schneiden**
slice (v)

**reiben**
grate (v)

**gießen**
pour (v)

**verrühren**
mix (v)

**schlagen**
whisk (v)

**kochen**
boil (v)

**braten**
fry (v)

**ausrollen**
roll (v)

**rühren**
stir (v)

**köcheln lassen**
simmer (v)

**pochieren**
poach (v)

**backen**
bake (v)

**braten**
roast (v)

**grillen**
broil (v)

---

# die Küchengeräte • kitchenware

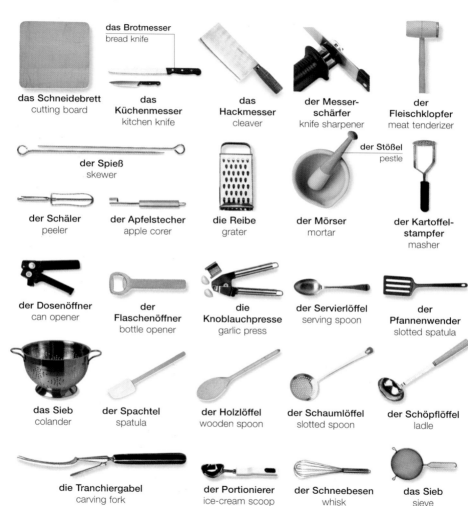

**das Schneidebrett**
cutting board

**das Brotmesser**
bread knife

**das Küchenmesser**
kitchen knife

**das Hackmesser**
cleaver

**der Messerschärfer**
knife sharpener

**der Fleischklopfer**
meat tenderizer

**der Spieß**
skewer

**der Schäler**
peeler

**der Apfelstecher**
apple corer

**die Reibe**
grater

**der Stößel**
pestle

**der Mörser**
mortar

**der Kartoffelstampfer**
masher

**der Dosenöffner**
can opener

**der Flaschenöffner**
bottle opener

**die Knoblauchpresse**
garlic press

**der Servierlöffel**
serving spoon

**der Pfannenwender**
slotted spatula

**das Sieb**
colander

**der Spachtel**
spatula

**der Holzlöffel**
wooden spoon

**der Schaumlöffel**
slotted spoon

**der Schöpflöffel**
ladle

**die Tranchiergabel**
carving fork

**der Portionierer**
ice-cream scoop

**der Schneebesen**
whisk

**das Sieb**
sieve

der Deckel
lid

kunststoffbeschichtet
nonstick

**die Bratpfanne**
frying pan

**der Kochtopf**
saucepan

**das Grillblech**
grill pan

**der Wok**
wok

**der Schmortopf**
earthenware dish

Glas-
glass

feuerfest
ovenproof

**die
Rührschüssel**
mixing bowl

**die Souffléform**
soufflé dish

**die Auflaufform**
gratin dish

**das
Auflaufförmchen**
ramekin

**die Kasserolle**
casserole dish

## das Kuchenbacken • baking cakes

**die
Haushaltswaage**
scale

**der Messbecher**
measuring cup

**die Kuchenform**
cake pan

**die
Pastetenform**
pie pan

**die Obstkuchen-
form**
quiche pan

**der Backpinsel**
pastry brush

**das Nudelholz**
rolling pin

**der Spritzbeutel**
piping bag

**die Törtchen-
form**
muffin pan

**das
Kuchenblech**
cookie sheet

**das Abkühlgitter**
cooling rack

**der
Topfhandschuh**
oven mitt

**die Schürze**
apron

# das Schlafzimmer • bedroom

**der Kleiderschrank**
wardrobe

**die Nachttisch lampe**
bedside lamp

**das Kopfende**
headboard

**der Nachttisch**
nightstand

**die Kommode**
chest of drawers

**die Schublade**
drawer

**das Bett**
bed

**die Matratze**
mattress

**die Tagesdecke**
bedspread

**das Kopfkissen**
pillow

**die Wärmflasche**
hot-water bottle

**der Radiowecker**
clock radio

**der Wecker**
alarm clock

**die Papiertaschen tuchschachtel**
box of tissues

**der Kleiderbügel**
coat hanger

## die Bettwäsche • bed linen

der Spiegel
mirror

der
Frisiertisch
dressing
table

der
Fußboden
floor

der Kissenbezug
pillowcase

das Bettlaken
sheet

der Volant
dust ruffle

die Bettdecke
comforter

die Steppdecke
quilt

die Decke
blanket

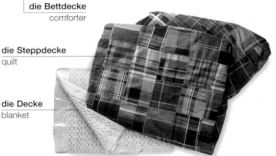

---

### Vokabular • vocabulary

| | | | | |
|---|---|---|---|---|
| **das Einzelbett**<br>twin bed | **das Fußende**<br>footboard | **der Teppich**<br>carpet | **einschlafen**<br>go to sleep (v) | **das Bett machen**<br>make the bed (v) |
| **das Doppelbett**<br>full bed | **der**<br>**Sprungrahmen**<br>bedspring | **die Schlaflosigkeit**<br>insomnia | **aufwachen**<br>wake up (v) | **den Wecker stellen**<br>set the alarm (v) |
| **die Heizdecke**<br>electric blanket | | **ins Bett gehen**<br>go to bed (v) | **aufstehen**<br>get up (v) | **schnarchen**<br>snore (v) |
| | | | | **der Einbauschrank**<br>closet |

---

# das Badezimmer • bathroom

der
**Handtuchhalter**
towel rack

**die Duschtür**
shower door

der
**Kaltwasserhahn**
cold faucet

der
**Heißwasserhahn**
hot faucet

das
**Waschbecken**
sink

der **Duschkopf**
shower head

die **Dusche**
shower

der **Stöpsel**
plug

der **Abfluss**
drain

der **Toilettensitz**
toilet seat

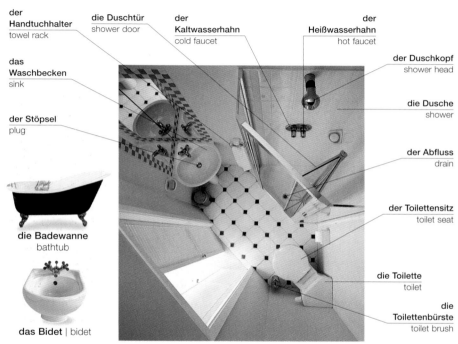

**die Badewanne**
bathtub

die **Toilette**
toilet

die
**Toilettenbürste**
toilet brush

**das Bidet** | bidet

**Vokabular** • vocabulary

**die Hausapotheke**
medicine cabinet

**die Bademisse**
bath mat

**die Bademtte**
bath mat

**die Rolle Toilettenpapier**
toilet paper

**der Duschvorhang**
shower curtain

**duschen**
take a shower (v)

**baden**
take a bath (v)

## die Zahnpflege • dental hygiene

**die Zahnbürste**
toothbrush

die
**Zahnseide**
dental floss

**die Zahnpasta**
toothpaste

**das Mundwasser**
mouthwash

**der Schwamm**
sponge

**der Bimsstein**
pumice stone

**die Rückenbürste**
back brush

**das Deo**
deodorant

die
**Seifenschale**
soap dish

**das Duschgel**
shower gel

**die Seife**
soap

**die Gesichtscreme**
face cream

**das Schaumbad**
bubble bath

**das Handtuch**
hand towel

das
**Badetuch**
bath towel

**die Handtücher**
towels

**die Körperlotion**
body lotion

**der Körperpuder**
talcum powder

**der Bademantel**
bathrobe

# das Rasieren • shaving

der
**Elektrorasierer**
electric razor

**der Rasierschaum**
shaving foam

**der Einwegrasierer**
disposable razor

die
**Rasierklinge**
razor blade

**das Rasierwasser**
aftershave

# das Kinderzimmer • nursery

## die Säuglingspflege • baby care

**die Wundsalbe**
diaper rash cream

**das Feuchttuch**
wet wipe

**der Schwamm**
sponge

**die Babywanne**
baby bath

**das Töpfchen**
potty

**die Wickelmatte**
changing mat

## das Schlafen • sleeping

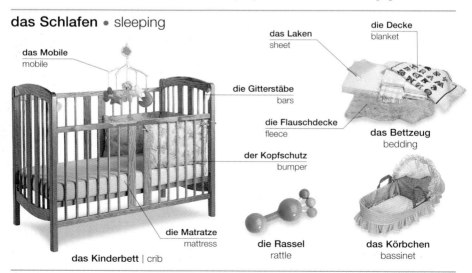

**das Mobile**
mobile

**das Laken**
sheet

**die Decke**
blanket

**die Gitterstäbe**
bars

**die Flauschdecke**
fleece

**das Bettzeug**
bedding

**der Kopfschutz**
bumper

**die Matratze**
mattress

**die Rassel**
rattle

**das Körbchen**
bassinet

**das Kinderbett** | crib

# das Spielen • playing

die Puppe
doll

**das Kuscheltier**
stuffed toy

**das Puppenhaus**
dollhouse

**das Spielhaus**
playhouse

# die Sicherheit • safety

die Kindersicherung
child lock

**das Babyphon**
baby monitor

der Teddy
teddy bear

das Spielzeug
toy

**der Spielzeugkorb**
toy basket

der Ball
ball

**der Laufstall**
playpen

**das Treppengitter**
stair gate

# das Essen • eating

**der Kinderstuhl**
high chair

der Sauger
nipple

die Schnabeltasse
drinking cup

**die Babyflasche**
bottle

# das Ausgehen • going out

**der Sportwagen**
stroller

das Verdeck
hood

**der Kinderwagen**
baby carriage

die Windel
diaper

**das Tragebettchen**
carrier

**die Babytasche**
diaper bag

**die Babytrageschlinge**
baby sling

# der Allzweckraum • utility room

## die Wäsche • laundry

**die saubere Wäsche**
clean clothes

**die schmutzige Wäsche**
dirty laundry

**der Wäschekorb**
laundry basket

**die Waschmaschine**
washing machine

**der Waschtrockner**
washer-dryer

**der Trockner**
tumble dryer

**die Wäscheleine**
clothesline

**das Bügeleisen**
iron

**die Wäsche klammer**
clothespin

**trocknen**
dry (v)

**das Bügelbrett** | ironing board

---

**Vokabular • vocabulary**

| | | | |
|---|---|---|---|
| **füllen** load (v) | **schleudern** spin (v) | **bügeln** iron (v) | **Wie benutze ich die Waschmaschine?** How do I operate the washing machine? |
| **spülen** rinse (v) | **die Wäscheschleuder** spin-dryer | **der Weichspüler** fabric softener | **Welches Programm nehme ich für farbige/weiße Wäsche?** What is the setting for colors/whites? |

---

# die Reinigungsartikel • cleaning equipment

der Saugschlauch
suction hose

der Handfeger
brush

die Müllschaufel
dustpan

das Reinigungsmittel
bleach

der Eimer
bucket

das Pulver
powder

der
Flüssigreiniger
liquid

das
Staubtuch
dust cloth

der Staubsauger
vacuum cleaner

der Mopp
mop

das Waschmittel
detergent

die Politur
polish

# die Tätigkeiten • activities

**putzen**
clean (v)

**spülen**
wash (v)

**wischen**
wipe (v)

**schrubben**
scrub (v)

**kratzen**
scrape (v)

der Besen
broom

**fegen**
sweep (v)

**Staub wischen**
dust (v)

**polieren**
polish (v)

# die Heimwerkstatt • workshop

das Bohrfutter
chuck

der Bohrer
drill bit

die Batterie
battery pack

**die Stichsäge**
jigsaw

**der Bohrer mit Batteriebetrieb**
cordless drill

**der Elektrobohrer**
electric drill

**die Leimpistole**
glue gun

die Zwinge
clamp

das Blatt
blade

**der Schraubstock**
vise

**die Schleifmaschine**
sander

**die Kreissäge**
circular saw

**die Werkbank**
workbench

der Holzleim
wood glue

das
Werkzeuggestell
tool rack

der Grundhobel
router

die Bohrwinde
bit brace

die Holzspäne
wood shavings

die
Verlängerungsschnur
extension cord

# die Techniken • techniques

**schneiden**
cut (v)

**sägen**
saw (v)

**bohren**
drill (v)

**hämmern**
hammer (v)

**hobeln**
plane (v)

**drechseln**
turn (v)

**schnitzen**
carve (v)

der Lötzinn
solder

**löten**
solder (v)

# die Materialien • materials

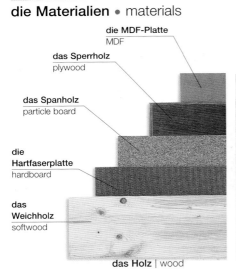

die MDF-Platte
MDF

das Sperrholz
plywood

das Spanholz
particle board

**die Hartfaserplatte**
hardboard

**das Weichholz**
softwood

**das Holz** | wood

das Hartholz
hardwood

der Lack
varnish

**die Beize**
wood stain

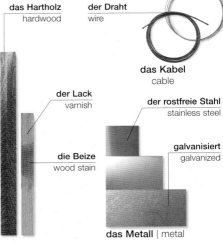

der Draht
wire

**das Kabel**
cable

der rostfreie Stahl
stainless steel

galvanisiert
galvanized

**das Metall** | metal

# der Werkzeugkasten • toolbox

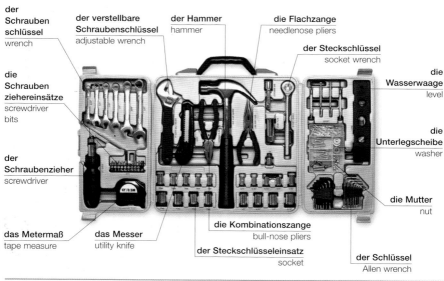

der
Schrauben
schlüssel
wrench

der verstellbare
Schraubenschlüssel
adjustable wrench

der Hammer
hammer

die Flachzange
needlenose pliers

der Steckschlüssel
socket wrench

die
Wasserwaage
level

die
Schrauben
ziehereinsätze
screwdriver
bits

die
Unterlegscheibe
washer

der
Schraubenzieher
screwdriver

die Mutter
nut

das Metermaß
tape measure

das Messer
utility knife

die Kombinationszange
bull-nose pliers

der Steckschlüsseleinsatz
socket

der Schlüssel
Allen wrench

# die Bohrer • drill bits

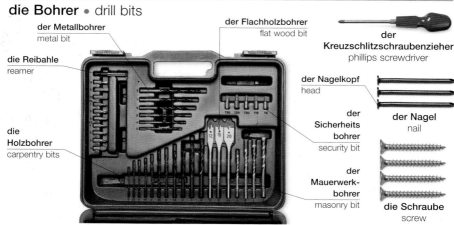

der Metallbohrer
metal bit

der Flachholzbohrer
flat wood bit

der
Kreuzschlitzschraubenzieher
phillips screwdriver

die Reibahle
reamer

der Nagelkopf
head

die
Holzbohrer
carpentry bits

der
Sicherheits
bohrer
security bit

der Nagel
nail

der
Mauerwerk-
bohrer
masonry bit

die Schraube
screw

die Entisolierzange
wire strippers

der Drahtschneider
wire cutters

das Isolierband
electrical tape

der Lötkolben
soldering iron

das Skalpell
craft knife

die Laubsäge
fretsaw

der Lötzinn
solder

die Profilsäge | tenon saw

die Schutzbrille
safety goggles

der Hobel
plane

die Gehrungslade
miter block

der Fuchsschwanz
handsaw

der Handbohrer
hand drill

die Stahlwolle
steel wool

das Schmirgelpapier
sandpaper

die Metallsäge
hacksaw

die Rohrzange
wrench

der Meißel
chisel

die Feile
file

der Wetzstahl
whetstone

der Rohrabschneider | pipe cutter

die Saugglocke
plunger

# das Tapezieren • decorating

**die Tapezierschere**
scissors

**das Tapeziermesser**
utility knife

**das Senkblei**
plumb line

**der Spachtel**
scraper

der
**Tapezierer**
decorator

**die Tapete**
wallpaper

**die Trittleiter**
stepladder

die
**Tapezierbürste**
wallpaper brush

der
**Tapeziertisch**
pasting table

die
**Kleisterbürste**
pasting brush

der
**Tapetenkleister**
wallpaper paste

**der Eimer**
bucket

**tapezieren** | wallpaper (v)

**abziehen**
strip (v)

**spachteln**
fill (v)

**schmirgeln**
sand (v)

**verputzen** | plaster (v)

**anbringen** | hang (v)

**kacheln** | tile (v)

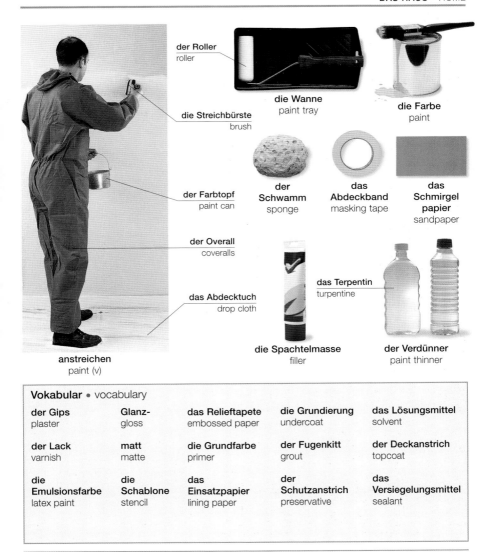

der Roller
roller

die Wanne
paint tray

die Farbe
paint

die Streichbürste
brush

der
Schwamm
sponge

das
Abdeckband
masking tape

das
Schmirgel
papier
sandpaper

der Farbtopf
paint can

der Overall
coveralls

das Terpentin
turpentine

das Abdecktuch
drop cloth

die Spachtelmasse
filler

der Verdünner
paint thinner

anstreichen
paint (v)

## Vokabular • vocabulary

| der Gips | Glanz- | das Relieftapete | die Grundierung | das Lösungsmittel |
|---|---|---|---|---|
| plaster | gloss | embossed paper | undercoat | solvent |
| der Lack | matt | die Grundfarbe | der Fugenkitt | der Deckanstrich |
| varnish | matte | primer | grout | topcoat |
| die Emulsionsfarbe | die Schablone | das Einsatzpapier | der Schutzanstrich | das Versiegelungsmittel |
| latex paint | stencil | lining paper | preservative | sealant |

# der Garten • garden

## die Gartentypen • garden styles

**der Patio**
patio garden

**der architektonische Garten** | formal garden

**der Bauerngarten**
cottage garden

**der Kräutergarten**
herb garden

**der Dachgarten**
roof garden

**der Steingarten**
rock garden

**der Hof**
courtyard

**der Wassergarten**
water garden

## die Garten ornamente • garden features

**die Blumenampel**
hanging basket

**das Spalier**
trellis

**die Pergola**
arbor

die Platten
paving

der Weg
path

der Kompost
haufen
compost pile

das Tor
gate

das
Blumenbeet
flowerbed

**der Boden** •
soil

die Erde
topsoil

der Sand
sand

der Kalk
chalk

der
Schuppen
shed

das
Gewächshaus
greenhouse

der Rasen
lawn

der Zaun
fence

der Schluff
silt

der Teich
pond

die Hecke
hedge

der Bogen
arch

der
Gemüsegarten
vegetable
garden

die Staudenrabatte
herbaceous border

der Lehm
clay

die Planken
deck

**der Springbrunnen** | fountain

# die Gartenpflanzen • garden plants

## die Pflanzenarten • types of plants

**einjährig**
annual

**zweijährig**
biennial

**mehrjährig**
perennial

**die Zwiebel**
bulb

**der Farn**
fern

**die Binse**
cattail

**der Bambus**
bamboo

**das Unkraut**
weeds

**das Kraut**
herb

**die Wasserpflanze**
water plant

**der Baum**
tree

**die Palme**
palm

**der Nadelbaum**
conifer

**immergrün**
evergreen

**der Laubbaum**
deciduous

**der Formschnitt**
topiary

**die Alpenpflanze**
alpine

**die Fettpflanze**
succulent

**der Kaktus**
cactus

**die Topfpflanze**
potted plant

**die Schattenpflanze**
shade plant

**die Kletterpflanze**
climber

**der Zierstrauch**
flowering shrub

**der Bodendecker**
ground cover

**die Kriechpflanze**
creeper

**Zier-**
ornamental

**das Gras**
grass

# die Gartengeräte • garden tools

**der Laubrechen**
lawn rake

**die Komposterde**
compost

**die Samen**
seeds

**die Knochenasche**
bone meal

**der Kies**
gravel

**der Spaten**
shovel

**die Gabel**
fork

**die Schere**
long-handled shears

**der Rechen**
rake

**die Hacke**
hoe

**der Grasfangsack**
grass bag

**der Motor**
motor

**der Griff**
handle

**der Gartenkorb**
gardening basket

**der Schutz**
shield

**der Ständer**
stand

**der Schneider**
trimmer

**der Rasenmäher**
lawnmower

**der Schubkarren**
wheelbarrow

**die Handgabel**
hand fork

**die Pflanzschaufel**
trowel

**die Rosenschere**
pruners

**die Gartenhandschuhe**
gardening gloves

**der Zwirn**
twine

die
**Pflanzenschildchen**
labels

**die Klinge**
blade

**der Setzkasten**
seed tray

die
**Befestigungen**
twist ties

die
**Ringbefestigungen**
ring ties

**die Garten
stöcke**
canes

**die Heckenschere**
shears

**das Sieb**
sieve

**das Pestizid**
pesticide

**der Blumentopf**
plant pot

**die Gummistiefel**
rubber boots

**die Handsäge**
hand saw

## Gießen • watering

**die Gartenspritze**
spray bottle

**der
Rasensprenger**
sprinkler

**die Düse**
nozzle

**die Gießkanne**
watering can

**der Gartenschlauch**
hose

**die Brause**
spray

**der Schlauchwagen** | hose reel

# die Gartenarbeit • gardening

der Rasen
lawn

das Blumenbeet
flowerbed

der Rasenmäher
lawnmower

die Hecke
hedge

die Stange
stake

**mähen** | mow (v)

**mit Rasen bedecken**
sod (v)

**stechen**
spike (v)

**harken**
rake (v)

**stutzen**
trim (v)

**graben**
dig (v)

**säen**
sow (v)

**mit Kopfdünger düngen**
top-dress (v)

**gießen**
water (v)

**ziehen**
train (v)

**köpfen**
deadhead (v)

**sprühen**
spray (v)

der Stock
cane

**hochbinden**
stake (v)

**pfropfen**
graft (v)

der Ableger
cutting

**vermehren**
propagate (v)

**beschneiden**
prune (v)

**umpflanzen**
transplant (v)

**jäten**
weed (v)

**mulchen**
mulch (v)

**ernten**
harvest (v)

---

**Vokabular • vocabulary**

| | | | | | | |
|---|---|---|---|---|---|---|
| **züchten** cultivate (v) | **gestalten** landscape (v) | **düngen** fertilize (v) | **sieben** sift (v) | **biodynamisch** organic | **die Entwässerung** drainage | **der Dünger** fertilizer |
| **hegen** tend (v) | **eintopfen** pot (v) | **pflücken** pick (v) | **auflockern** aerate (v) | **der Untergrund** subsoil | **der Unkrautvernichter** weedkiller | **der Sämling** seedling |

---

# die Dienstleistungen
services

# die Notdienste • emergency services

## der Rettungsdienst • ambulance

die Tragbahre
stretcher

der Krankenwagen
ambulance

der Rettungssanitäter
paramedic

## die Polizei • police

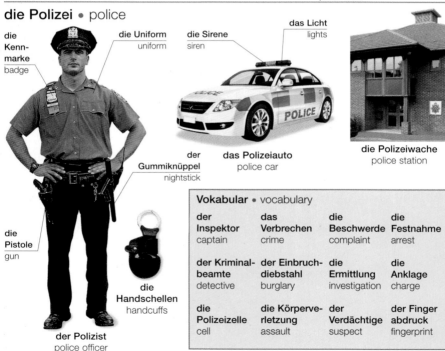

die Kenn-marke
badge

die Uniform
uniform

die Sirene
siren

das Licht
lights

der Gummiknüppel
nightstick

das Polizeiauto
police car

die Polizeiwache
police station

die Pistole
gun

die Handschellen
handcuffs

der Polizist
police officer

| Vokabular • vocabulary | | | |
|---|---|---|---|
| der Inspektor captain | das Verbrechen crime | die Beschwerde complaint | die Festnahme arrest |
| der Kriminal-beamte detective | der Einbruch-diebstahl burglary | die Ermittlung investigation | die Anklage charge |
| die Polizeizelle cell | die Körperve-rletzung assault | der Verdächtige suspect | der Finger abdruck fingerprint |

# die Feuerwehr • fire department

der Schutzhelm
helmet

der Rauch
smoke

der Schlauch
hose

der Auslegerkorb
basket

die Feuerwehrleute
firefighters

der Wasserstrahl
water jet

die Fahrerkabine
cab

der Ausleger
boom

die Leiter
ladder

der Brand | fire

die Feuerwache
fire station

die Feuertreppe
fire escape

das Löschfahrzeug
fire engine

der Rauchmelder
smoke alarm

der Feuermelder
fire alarm

das Beil
ax

der Feuerlöscher
fire extinguisher

der Hydrant
hydrant

| Die Polizei/die Feuerwehr/einen Krankenwagen, bitte. I need the police/fire department/ambulance. | Es brennt in… There's a fire at… | Es ist ein Unfall passiert. There's been an accident. | Rufen Sie die Polizei! Call the police! |
| --- | --- | --- | --- |

# die Bank • bank

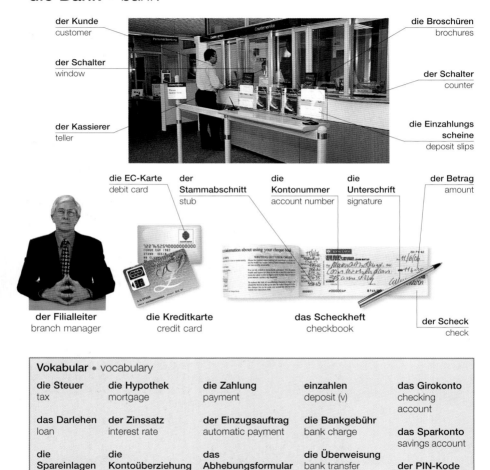

der Kunde
customer

der Schalter
window

der Kassierer
teller

die Broschüren
brochures

der Schalter
counter

die Einzahlungs
scheine
deposit slips

die EC-Karte
debit card

der
Stammabschnitt
stub

die
Kontonummer
account number

die
Unterschrift
signature

der Betrag
amount

der Filialleiter
branch manager

die Kreditkarte
credit card

das Scheckheft
checkbook

der Scheck
check

---

**Vokabular • vocabulary**

| | | | | |
|---|---|---|---|---|
| die Steuer<br>tax | die Hypothek<br>mortgage | die Zahlung<br>payment | einzahlen<br>deposit (v) | das Girokonto<br>checking<br>account |
| das Darlehen<br>loan | der Zinssatz<br>interest rate | der Einzugsauftrag<br>automatic payment | die Bankgebühr<br>bank charge | das Sparkonto<br>savings account |
| die<br>Spareinlagen<br>savings | die<br>Kontoüberziehung<br>overdraft | das<br>Abhebungsformular<br>withdrawal slip | die Überweisung<br>bank transfer | der PIN-Kode<br>PIN |

---

die Münze
coin

der Schein
bill

der
Bildschirm
screen

das
Tastenfeld
keypad

der
Kartenschlitz
card reader

das Geld
money

der Geldautomat
ATM

## die ausländische Währung •
foreign currency

die Wechselstube
currency exchange

der Reisescheck
traveler's check

der Wechselkurs
exchange rate

## die Geldwirtschaft • finance

der Aktienpreis
share price

der
Börsenmakler
stockbroker

die Finanzberaterin
financial advisor

die Börse | stock exchange

| **Vokabular** • vocabulary | |
|---|---|
| einlösen cash (v) | die Aktien shares |
| der Nennwert denomination | die Gewinnanteile dividends |
| die Provision commission | das Portefeuille portfolio |
| die Wertpapiere stocks | das Eigenkapital equity |
| die Kapitalanlage investment | der Buchhalter accountant |

**Könnte ich das bitte wechseln?**
Can I change this, please?

**Wie ist der heutige Wechselkurs?**
What's today's exchange rate?

# die Kommunikation • communications

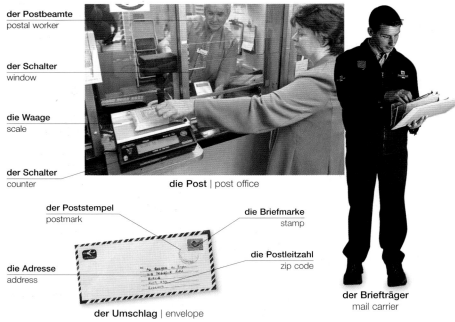

**der Postbeamte**
postal worker

**der Schalter**
window

**die Waage**
scale

**der Schalter**
counter

**die Post** | post office

**der Poststempel**
postmark

**die Briefmarke**
stamp

**die Postleitzahl**
zip code

**die Adresse**
address

**der Umschlag** | envelope

**der Briefträger**
mail carrier

**Vokabular** • vocabulary

| | | | | |
|---|---|---|---|---|
| **der Brief**<br>letter | **der Absender**<br>return address | **die Zustellung**<br>delivery | **zerbrechlich**<br>fragile | **nicht falten**<br>do not bend (v) |
| **per Luftpost**<br>by airmail | **die Unterschrift**<br>signature | **die Postgebühr**<br>postage | **der Postsack**<br>mailbag | **oben**<br>this way up |
| **das Einschreiben**<br>registered mail | **die Leerung**<br>pickup | **die Postanweisung**<br>money order | **das Telegramm**<br>telegram | |

**der Briefkasten**
mailbox

**der Hausbriefkasten**
letter slot

**das Paket**
package

**der Kurierdienst**
courier

## das Telefon • telephone

**der Hörer**
handset

**der Anrufbeantworter**
answering machine

**die Basis**
base station

**das schnurlose Telefon**
cordless phone

**das Bildtelefon**
video phone

**die Telefonzelle**
phone booth

**das Smartphone**
smartphone

**das Handy**
cell phone

**das Tastenfeld**
keypad

**der Hörer**
receiver

**die Münzrückgabe**
coin return

**der Münzfernsprecher**
payphone

---

**Vokabular** • vocabulary

**abheben**
answer (v)

**wählen**
dial (v)

**das R-Gespräch**
collect call

**die App**
app

**die Auskunft**
directory assistance

**die SMS**
text (SMS)

**die Sprachmitteilung**
voice message

**besetzt**
busy

**unterbrochen**
disconnected

**die Vermittlung**
operator

**der Passcode**
passcode

**Können Sie mir die Nummer für…geben?**
Can you give me the number for…?

**Was ist die Vorwahl für…?**
What is the area code for…?

**Schick mir eine SMS!**
Text me!

---

# das Hotel • hotel
## die Empfangshalle • lobby

**der Gast**
guest

**der Zimmerschlüssel**
room key

**die Nachrichten**
messages

**das Fach**
pigeonhole

**die Empfangsdame**
receptionist

**das Gästebuch**
register

**der Schalter**
counter

**der Empfang** | reception

**das Gepäck**
luggage

**der Kofferkuli**
cart

**der Page**
porter

**der Fahrstuhl**
elevator

**die Zimmernummer**
room number

## die Zimmer • rooms

**das Einzelzimmer**
single room

**das Doppelzimmer**
double room

**das Zweibettzimmer**
twin room

**das Privatbadezimmer**
private bathroom

# die Dienstleistungen • services

**die Zimmerreinigung**
maid service

**der Wäschedienst**
laundry service

**das Frühstückstablett**
breakfast tray

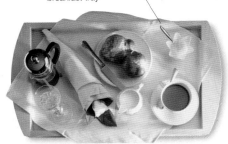

**der Zimmerservice** | room service

**die Minibar**
minibar

**das Restaurant**
restaurant

**der Fitnessraum**
gym

**das Schwimmbad**
swimming pool

---

**Vokabular** • vocabulary

**die Vollpension**
all meals included

**die Halbpension**
some meals included

**die Übernachtung mit Frühstück**
bed and breakfast

**Haben Sie ein Zimmer frei?**
Do you have any vacancies?

**Ich möchte ein Einzelzimmer.**
I'd like a single room.

**Ich habe ein Zimmer reserviert.**
I have a reservation.

**Ich möchte ein Zimmer für drei Nächte.**
I'd like a room for three nights.

**Was kostet das Zimmer pro Nacht?**
What is the charge per night?

**Wann muss ich das Zimmer räumen?**
When do I have to check out?

---

**der Einkauf**
shopping

# das Einkaufszentrum • shopping center

**das Atrium**
atrium

**das Schild**
sign

**der Fahrstuhl**
elevator

**die zweite Etage**
third floor

**die erste Etage**
second floor

**die Rolltreppe**
escalator

**das Erdgeschoss**
ground floor

**der Kunde**
customer

## Vokabular • vocabulary

| | | | |
|---|---|---|---|
| **die Kinderabteilung**<br>children's department | **der Kundendienst**<br>customer services | **die Anprobe**<br>fitting rooms | **Was kostet das?**<br>How much is this? |
| **die Gepäckabteilung**<br>luggage department | **die Anzeigetafel**<br>store directory | **der Wickelraum**<br>baby changing room | **Kann ich das umtauschen?**<br>May I exchange this? |
| **die Schuhabteilung**<br>shoe department | **der Verkäufer**<br>salesclerk | **die Toiletten**<br>restroom | |

# das Kaufhaus • department store

**die Herrenbekleidung**
menswear

**die Damenoberbekleidung**
womenswear

**die Damenwäsche**
lingerie

**die Parfümerie**
perfumes

**die Schönheitspflege**
cosmetics

**die Wäsche**
linens

**die Möbel**
home furnishings

**die Kurzwaren**
notions

**die Küchengeräte**
kitchenware

**das Porzellan**
china

**die Elektroartikel**
electronics

**die Lampen**
lighting

**die Sportartikel**
sportswear

**die Spielwaren**
toys

**die Schreibwaren**
stationery

**die Lebensmittelabteilung**
groceries

# der Supermarkt • supermarket

**der Gang**
aisle

**das Warenregal**
shelf

**das Laufband**
conveyer belt

**der Kassierer**
checker

**die Angebote**
specials

**die Kasse** | checkout

**der Kunde**
customer

**die Kasse**
cash register

**die Einkaufstasche**
shopping bag

**die Lebensmittel**
groceries

**der Henkel**
handle

**der Strichcode**
bar code

**der Einkaufswagen**
grocery cart

**der Einkaufskorb**
basket

**der Scanner**
scanner

**die Backwaren**
bakery

**die Milchprodukte**
dairy

**die Getreideflocken**
breakfast cereals

**die Konserven**
canned food

**die Süßwaren**
candy

**das Gemüse**
vegetables

**das Obst**
fruit

**das Fleisch und das Geflügel**
meat and poultry

**der Fisch**
fish

**die Feinkost**
deli

**die Gefrierware**
frozen food

**die Fertiggerichte**
prepared food

**die Getränke**
drinks

**die Haushaltswaren**
household products

**die Toilettenartikel**
toiletries

**die Babyprodukte**
baby products

**die Elektroartikel**
electrical goods

**das Tierfutter**
pet food

**die Zeitschriften** | magazines

# die Apotheke • drugstore

**die Zahnpflege**
dental care

**die Monats-hygiene**
feminine hygiene

**die Deos**
deodorants

**die Vitamintabletten**
vitamins

**die Apotheke**
pharmacy

**der Apotheker**
pharmacist

**das Hustenmedikament**
cough medicine

**das Kräuterheilmittel**
herbal remedies

**die Hautpflege**
skin care

**die Sonnenschutzcreme**
sunscreen

**die After-Sun-Lotion**
aftersun lotion

**der Sonnenblock**
sunblock

**das Insektenschutzmittel**
insect repellent

**das Reinigungstuch**
wet wipe

**das Papiertaschentuch**
tissue

**die Damenbinde**
sanitary napkin

**der Tampon**
tampon

**die Slipeinlage**
panty liner

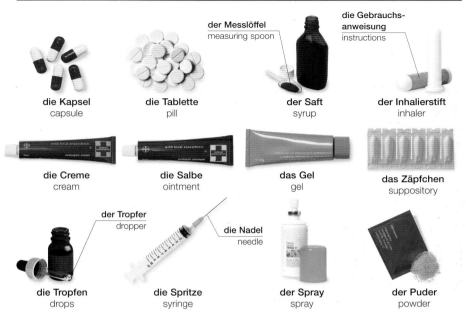

**der Messlöffel**
measuring spoon

**die Gebrauchs-anweisung**
instructions

**die Kapsel**
capsule

**die Tablette**
pill

**der Saft**
syrup

**der Inhalierstift**
inhaler

**die Creme**
cream

**die Salbe**
ointment

**das Gel**
gel

**das Zäpfchen**
suppository

**der Tropfer**
dropper

**die Nadel**
needle

**die Tropfen**
drops

**die Spritze**
syringe

**der Spray**
spray

**der Puder**
powder

**Vokabular** • vocabulary

| | | | | |
|---|---|---|---|---|
| **das Eisen**<br>iron | **das Multivitaminmittel**<br>multivitamins | **Wegwerf-**<br>disposable | **das Medikament**<br>medicine | **das Schmerzmittel**<br>painkiller |
| **das Kalzium**<br>calcium | **die Nebenwirkungen**<br>side effects | **löslich**<br>soluble | **der Durchfall**<br>diarrhea | **das Beruhigungsmittel**<br>sedative |
| **das Insulin**<br>insulin | **das Verfallsdatum**<br>expiration date | **die Dosierung**<br>dosage | **die Halspastille**<br>throat lozenge | **die Schlaftablette**<br>sleeping pill |
| **das Magnesium**<br>magnesium | **die Reisekrankheitstabletten**<br>travel-sickness pills | **die Verordnung**<br>medication | **das Abführmittel**<br>laxative | **der Entzündungshemmer**<br>anti-inflammatory |

# das Blumengeschäft • florist

die Blumen
flowers

die Gladiole
gladiolus

die Lilie
lily

die Iris
iris

die Akazie
acacia

die Margerite
daisy

die Chrysantheme
chrysanthemum

die Nelke
carnation

das Schleierkraut
gypsophila

die Topfpflanze
potted plant

| die Levkoje | die Gerbera | die Blätter | die Rose | die Freesie |
| --- | --- | --- | --- | --- |
| stocks | gerbera | foliage | rose | freesia |

die
**Blumenvase**
vase

**die Orchidee**
orchid

**die Pfingstrose**
peony

**der Strauß**
bunch

**der Stengel**
stem

**die Osterglocke**
daffodil

**die Knospe**
bud

das **Ein
wickelpapier**
wrapping

**die Tulpe** | tulip

# die Blumenarrangements • arrangements

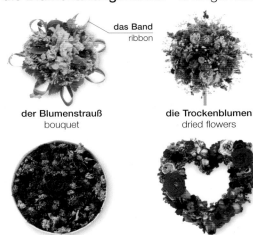

**das Band**
ribbon

**der Blumenstrauß**
bouquet

**die Trockenblumen**
dried flowers

**das Duftsträußchen** | potpourri

**der Kranz** | wreath

die
**Blumengirlande**
garland

| **Vokabular** • vocabulary | |
| --- | --- |
| **Ich möchte einen Strauß… bitte.**<br>Can I have a bunch of… please. | **Wie lange halten sie?**<br>How long will these last? |
| **Können Sie die Blumen bitte einwickeln?**<br>Can I have them wrapped? | **Duften sie?**<br>Are they fragrant? |
| **Kann ich eine Nachricht mitschicken?**<br>Can I attach a message? | **Können Sie die Blumen an…schicken?**<br>Can you send them to…? |

# der Zeitungshändler • newsstand

**die Zigaretten**
cigarettes

**das Päckchen Zigaretten**
pack of cigarettes

**die Briefmarken**
stamps

**die Postkarte**
postcard

**das Comicheft**
comic book

**die Zeitschrift**
magazine

**die Zeitung**
newspaper

# das Rauchen • smoking

**das Mundstück**
stem

**der Kopf**
bowl

**der Tabak**
tobacco

**das Feuerzeug**
lighter

**die Pfeife**
pipe

**die Zigarre**
cigar

# der Süßwarenhändler • candy store

**die Schachtel Pralinen**
box of chocolates

**die Nascherei**
snack bar

**die Chips**
potato chips

**das Süßwarengeschäft** | candy store

**Vokabular** • vocabulary

**die Milchschokolade**
milk chocolate

**die bittere Schokolade**
dark chocolate

**die weiße Schokolade**
white chocolate

**die bunte Mischung**
pick and mix

**der Karamell**
caramel

**der Trüffel**
truffle

**der Keks**
cookie

## die Süßwaren • confectionery

**die Praline**
chocolate

**die Tafel Schokolade**
chocolate bar

**die Bonbons**
hard candy

**der Lutscher**
lollipop

**das Toffee**
toffee

**der Nugat**
nougat

**das Marshmallow**
marshmallow

**das Pfefferminz**
mint

**der Kaugummi**
chewing gum

**der Geleebonbon**
jellybean

**der Fruchtgummi**
gumdrop

**die Lakritze**
licorice

# andere Geschäfte • other stores

**die Bäckerei**
bakery

**die Konditorei**
pastry shop

**die Metzgerei**
butcher shop

**das Fischgeschäft**
fish counter

**der Gemüseladen**
produce stand

**das Lebensmittelgeschäft**
grocery store

**das Schuhgeschäft**
shoe store

**die Eisenwaren-handlung**
hardware store

**der Antiquitätenladen**
antique store

**der Geschenkartikel-laden**
gift shop

**das Reisebüro**
travel agency

**das Juweliergeschäft**
jewelry store

**der Buchladen**
bookstore

**das Musikgeschäft**
record store

**die Weinhandlung**
liquor store

**die Tierhandlung**
pet store

**das Möbelgeschäft**
furniture store

**die Boutique**
boutique

**Vokabular** • vocabulary

| | |
|---|---|
| **das Gartencenter**<br>garden center | **das Fotogeschäft**<br>camera store |
| **die Reinigung**<br>dry cleaner | **das Reformhaus**<br>health food store |
| **der Waschsalon**<br>laundromat | **die Kunsthandlung**<br>art supply store |
| **der Immobilienmakler**<br>real estate office | **der Gebrauchtwarenhändler**<br>secondhand store |

**die Schneiderei**
tailor shop

**der Frisiersalon**
salon

**der Markt** | market

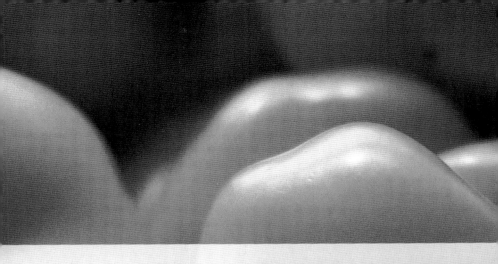

**die Nahrungsmittel**
food

# das Fleisch • meat

das Lamm
lamb

der Metzger
butcher

der Fleischerhaken
meat hook

die Waage
scale

der Messerschärfer
knife sharpener

der Speck
bacon

die Würstchen
sausages

die Leber
liver

## Vokabular • vocabulary

| | | | | |
|---|---|---|---|---|
| **das Rindfleisch**<br>beef | **das Wild**<br>venison | **die Zunge**<br>tongue | **aus Freilandhaltung**<br>free range | **das rote Fleisch**<br>red meat |
| **das Kalbfleisch**<br>veal | **das Kaninchen**<br>rabbit | **gepökelt**<br>cured | **biologisch kontrolliert**<br>organic | **das magere Fleisch**<br>lean meat |
| **das Schweinefleisch**<br>pork | **die Innereien**<br>variety meat | **geräuchert**<br>smoked | **das weiße Fleisch**<br>white meat | **das gekochte Fleisch**<br>cooked meat |

# die Fleischsorten • cuts

**die Scheibe**
slice

**die Speckscheibe**
bacon strip

**das Hackfleisch**
ground meat

**das Filet**
fillet

**das Rumpsteak**
rump steak

der Schinken
ham

die
Schwarte
rind

das Fett
fat

der
Knochen
bone

die Niere
kidney

**das Lendensteak**
sirloin steak

**das Rippenstück**
rib

**das Kotelett**
chop

**die Keule**
joint

**das Herz**
heart

# das Geflügel • poultry

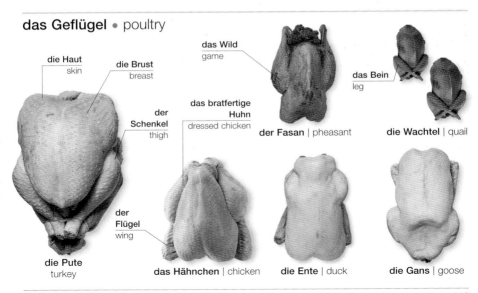

die Haut
skin

die Brust
breast

das Wild
game

das Bein
leg

der
Schenkel
thigh

das bratfertige
Huhn
dressed chicken

**der Fasan** | pheasant

**die Wachtel** | quail

der
Flügel
wing

**die Pute**
turkey

**das Hähnchen** | chicken

**die Ente** | duck

**die Gans** | goose

# der Fisch • fish

die geschälten Garnelen
peeled shrimp

die rote Meerbarbe
red mullet

die Heilbuttfilets
halibut fillets

die Regenbogenforelle
rainbow trout

das Eis
ice

die Rochenflügel
skate wings

das Fischgeschäft
fish counter

die Quappe
monkfish

die Makrele
mackerel

die Forelle
trout

der Schwertfisch
swordfish

die Seezunge
Dover sole

die Rotzunge
lemon sole

der Schellfisch
haddock

die Sardine
sardine

der Rochen
skate

der Merlan
whiting

der Seebarsch
sea bass

der Lachs | salmon

der Kabeljau
cod

der Seebrassen
sea bream

der Tunfisch
tuna

# die Meeresfrüchte • seafood

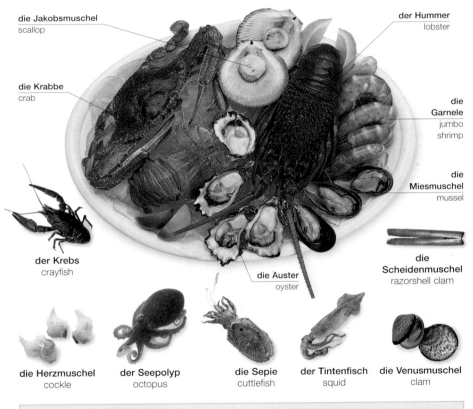

die Jakobsmuschel
scallop

der Hummer
lobster

die Krabbe
crab

die Garnele
jumbo shrimp

die Miesmuschel
mussel

der Krebs
crayfish

die Scheidenmuschel
razorshell clam

die Auster
oyster

die Herzmuschel
cockle

der Seepolyp
octopus

die Sepie
cuttlefish

der Tintenfisch
squid

die Venusmuschel
clam

## Vokabular • vocabulary

| | | | | | | | |
|---|---|---|---|---|---|---|---|
| tiefgefroren frozen | gesalzen salted | gesäubert cleaned | entschuppt scaled | enthäutet skinned | das Loin loin | die Gräte bone | das Filet fillet |
| frisch fresh | geräuchert smoked | filetiert filleted | entgrätet boned | die Schuppe scale | der Schwanz tail | die Schnitte steak | Können Sie ihn mir säubern? Will you clean it for me? |

# das Gemüse 1 • vegetables 1

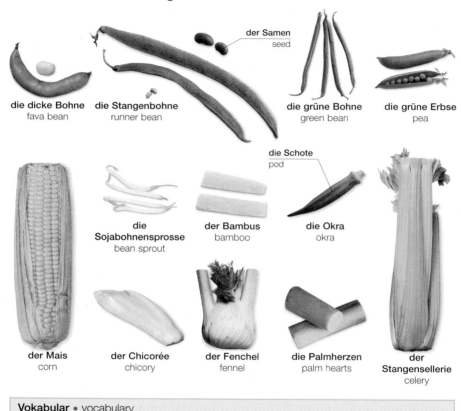

der Samen
seed

**die dicke Bohne**
fava bean

**die Stangenbohne**
runner bean

**die grüne Bohne**
green bean

**die grüne Erbse**
pea

die Schote
pod

**die
Sojabohnensprosse**
bean sprout

**der Bambus**
bamboo

**die Okra**
okra

**der Mais**
corn

**der Chicorée**
chicory

**der Fenchel**
fennel

**die Palmherzen**
palm hearts

**der
Stangensellerie**
celery

---

**Vokabular** • vocabulary

| | | | | |
|---|---|---|---|---|
| **das Blatt**<br>leaf | **das Röschen**<br>floret | **die Spitze**<br>tip | **biologisch**<br>organic | **Verkaufen Sie Biogemüse?**<br>Do you sell organic vegetables? |
| **der Strunk**<br>stalk | **der Kern**<br>kernel | **das Herz**<br>heart | **die Plastiktüte**<br>plastic bag | **Werden sie in dieser Gegend angebaut?**<br>Are these grown locally? |

**die Rauke**
arugula

**die Brunnenkresse**
watercress

**der Radicchio**
radicchio

**der Rosenkohl**
Brussels sprout

**der Mangold**
Swiss chard

**der Grünkohl**
kale

**der Garten-Sauerampfer**
sorrel

**die Endivie**
endive

**der Löwenzahn**
dandelion

**der Spinat**
spinach

**der Kohlrabi**
kohlrabi

**der Chinakohl**
bok choy

**der Salat**
lettuce

**der Brokkoli**
broccoli

**der Kohl**
cabbage

**der Frühkohl**
spring greens

# das Gemüse 2 • vegetables 2

**die Rübe**
turnip

**die Artischocke**
artichoke

**das Radieschen**
radish

**der Blumenkohl**
cauliflower

**die Kartoffel**
potato

**der Spargel**
asparagus

**der Gartenkürbis**
squash

**die Zwiebel**
onion

**die Paprika**
pepper

**die Peperoni**
chili pepper

**der Mais**
sweetcorn

---

**Vokabular • vocabulary**

| | | | | |
|---|---|---|---|---|
| **die Kirschtomate**<br>cherry tomato | **der Sellerie**<br>celeriac | **tiefgefroren**<br>frozen | **bitter**<br>bitter | **Könnte ich bitte ein Kilo Kartoffeln haben?**<br>Can I have one kilo of potatoes, please? |
| **die Karotte**<br>carrot | **die Tarowurzel**<br>taro root | **roh**<br>raw | **fest**<br>firm | |
| **die Brotfrucht**<br>breadfruit | **der Maniok**<br>cassava | **scharf**<br>hot (spicy) | **das Fleisch**<br>flesh | **Was kostet ein Kilo?**<br>What's the price per kilo? |
| **die neue Kartoffel**<br>new potato | **die Wasserkastanie**<br>water chestnut | **süß**<br>sweet | **die Wurzel**<br>root | **Wie heißen diese?**<br>What are those called? |

---

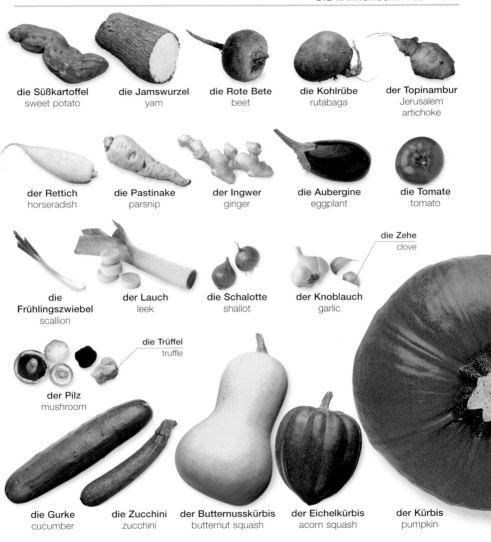

**die Süßkartoffel**
sweet potato

**die Jamswurzel**
yam

**die Rote Bete**
beet

**die Kohlrübe**
rutabaga

**der Topinambur**
Jerusalem
artichoke

**der Rettich**
horseradish

**die Pastinake**
parsnip

**der Ingwer**
ginger

**die Aubergine**
eggplant

**die Tomate**
tomato

**die
Frühlingszwiebel**
scallion

**der Lauch**
leek

**die Schalotte**
shallot

**die Zehe**
clove

**der Knoblauch**
garlic

**die Trüffel**
truffle

**der Pilz**
mushroom

**die Gurke**
cucumber

**die Zucchini**
zucchini

**der Butternusskürbis**
butternut squash

**der Eichelkürbis**
acorn squash

**der Kürbis**
pumpkin

# das Obst 1 • fruit 1

## die Zitrusfrüchte • citrus fruit

**die Orange**
orange

**die Klementine**
clementine

**die Tangelo**
ugli fruit

die weiße
**Haut**
pith

**die Grapefruit**
grapefruit

**die Mandarine**
tangerine

der Schnitz
segment

**die Satsuma**
satsuma

**die Schale**
zest

**die Limone**
lime

**die Zitrone**
lemon

**die Kumquat**
kumquat

## das Steinobst • stone fruit

**der Pfirsich**
peach

**die Nektarine**
nectarine

**die Aprikose**
apricot

**die Pflaume**
plum

**die Kirsche**
cherry

der Apfel
apple

die Birne
pear

**der Obstkorb** | basket of fruit

# das Beerenobst und die Melonen • berries and melons

**die Erdbeere**
strawberry

**die Himbeere**
raspberry

**die Melone**
melon

**die Weintrauben**
grapes

**die Brombeere**
blackberry

**die Johannisbeere**
red currant

**die Preiselbeere**
cranberry

**die schwarze
Johannisbeere**
black currant

die Schale
rind

der Kern
seed

das
Fruchtfleisch
flesh

 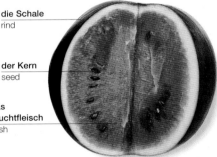

**die Wassermelone**
watermelon

**die Heidelbeere**
blueberry

**die weiße Johannisbeere**
white currant

**die Loganbeere**
loganberry

**die Stachelbeere**
gooseberry

## Vokabular • vocabulary

| | | | | |
|---|---|---|---|---|
| **saftig** juicy | **sauer** sour | **knackig** crisp | **kernlos** seedless | **Sind sie reif?** Are they ripe? |
| **die Faser** fiber | **frisch** fresh | **faul** rotten | **der Saft** juice | **Könnte ich eine probieren?** Can I try one? |
| **süß** sweet | **der Rhabarber** rhubarb | **das Fruchtmark** pulp | **das Kerngehäuse** core | **Wie lange halten sie sich?** How long will they keep? |

# das Obst 2 • fruit 2

die Mango
mango

die Ananas
pineapple

die Avocado
avocado

die Papaya
papaya

der Pfirsich
peach

die Litschi
lychee

die Kiwi
kiwifruit

die Kapstachelbeere
Cape gooseberry

der Kern
seed

die Schale
peel

**die Quitte**
quince

**die Passionsfrucht**
passion fruit

**die Banane**
banana

**die Guave**
guava

**der Granatapfel**
pomegranate

**die Kaki**
persimmon

**die Feijoa**
feijoa

**die Kaktusfeige**
prickly pear

**die Sternfrucht**
star fruit

**die Tamarillo**
tamarillo

# die Nüsse und das Dörrobst • nuts and dried fruit

**die Piniennuss**
pine nut

**die Pistazie**
pistachio

**die Cashewnuss**
cashew

**die Erdnuss**
peanut

**die Haselnuss**
hazelnut

**die Paranuss**
Brazil nut

**die Pecannuss**
pecan

**die Mandel**
almond

**die Walnuss**
walnut

**die Esskastanie**
chestnut

**die Macadamianuss**
macadamia

**die Feige**
fig

**die Dattel**
date

**die Backpflaume**
prune

die Schale
shell

**die Sultanine**
sultana

**die Rosine**
raisin

**die Korinthe**
currant

das
Fruchtfleisch
flesh

**die Kokosnuss**
coconut

---

**Vokabular** • vocabulary

| | | | | | | |
|---|---|---|---|---|---|---|
| **grün** green | **hart** hard | **der Kern** kernel | **gesalzen** salted | **geröstet** roasted | **die Südfrüchte** tropical fruit | **geschält** shelled |
| **reif** ripe | **weich** soft | **getrocknet** desiccated | **roh** raw | **Saison-** seasonal | **die kandierten Früchte** candied fruit | **ganz** whole |

---

# die Getreidearten und die Hülsenfrüchte •
## grains and legumes

### das Getreide • grains

**der Weizen**
wheat

**der Hafer**
oats

**die Gerste**
barley

**die Hirse**
millet

**der Mais**
corn

**die Reismelde**
quinoa

| Vokabular • vocabulary | | |
|---|---|---|
| **trocken** dry | **frisch** fresh | **Vollkorn** whole-grain |
| **die Hülse** husk | **aromatisch** fragranced | **Langkorn** long-grain |
| **der Kern** kernel | **einweichen** soak (v) | **Rundkorn** short-grain |
| **der Samen** seed | **die Getreideflocken** cereal | **leicht zu kochen** quick cooking |

### der Reis • rice

**der weiße Reis**
white rice

**der Naturreis**
brown rice

**der Wasserreis**
wild rice

**der Milchreis**
arborio rice

### die verarbeiteten Getreidearten •
processed grains

**der Kuskus**
couscous

**der Weizenschrot**
cracked wheat

**der Grieß**
semolina

**die Kleie**
bran

# die Hülsenfrüchte • beans and peas

**die Mondbohnen**
butter beans

**die weißen Bohnen**
haricot beans

**die roten Bohnen**
red kidney beans

**die Adzuki-bohnen**
adzuki beans

**die Saubohnen**
fava beans

**die Sojabohnen**
soybeans

**die Augenbohnen**
black-eyed peas

**die Pintobohnen**
pinto beans

**die Mungbohnen**
mung beans

**die französischen Bohnen**
flageolet beans

**die braunen Linsen**
brown lentils

**die roten Linsen**
red lentils

**die grünen Erbsen**
green peas

**die Kichererbsen**
chickpeas

**die getrockneten Erbsen**
split peas

# die Körner • seeds

**der Kürbiskern**
pumpkin seed

**das Senfkorn**
mustard seed

**der Kümmel**
caraway

**das Sesamkorn**
sesame seed

**der Sonnenblumenkern**
sunflower seed

# die Kräuter und Gewürze • herbs and spices

## die Gewürze • spices

**die Vanille**
vanilla

**die Muskatnuss**
nutmeg

**die Muskatblüte**
mace

**die Gelbwurz**
turmeric

**der Kreuzkümmel**
cumin

**die Kräutermischung**
bouquet garni

**der Piment**
allspice

**das Pfefferkorn**
peppercorn

**der Bockshornklee**
fenugreek

**der Chili**
chili powder

ganz
whole

zerstoßen
crushed

**der Safran**
saffron

**der Kardamom**
cardamom

**das Currypulver**
curry powder

gemahlen
ground

**der Paprika**
paprika

geraspelt
flakes

**der Knoblauch**
garlic

## die Kräuter • herbs

**die Stangen**
sticks

**der Zimt**
cinnamon

**der Fenchel**
fennel

**die Fenchelsamen**
fennel seeds

**das Lorbeerblatt**
bay leaf

**die Petersilie**
parsley

**das Zitronengras**
lemon grass

**die Gewürznelke**
cloves

**der Schnittlauch**
chives

**die Minze**
mint

**der Thymian**
thyme

**der Salbei**
sage

**der Sternanis**
star anise

**der Estragon**
tarragon

**der Majoran**
marjoram

**das Basilikum**
basil

**der Ingwer**
ginger

**der Oregano**
oregano

**der Koriander**
cilantro

**der Dill**
dill

**der Rosmarin**
rosemary

# die Nahrungsmittel in Flaschen •
bottled foods

das Walnussöl
walnut oil

das Traubenkernöl
grapeseed oil

der Korken
cork

das
Sonnenblumenöl
sunflower oil

das
Mandelöl
almond oil

das
Sesamöl
sesame
seed oil

das Haselnussöl
hazelnut oil

das Olivenöl
olive oil

die Kräuter
herbs

das
aromatische Öl
flavored oil

die Öle
oils

# der süße Aufstrich • sweet spreads

das Glas
jar

die Honigwabe
honeycomb

der feste Honig
set honey

der
Zitronenaufstrich
lemon curd

die
Himbeerkonfitüre
raspberry jam

die
Orangenmarmelade
marmalade

der flüssige
Honig
clear honey

der Ahornsirup
maple syrup

## die Soßen und die Kondimente •
sauces and condiments

der
**Apfelweinessig**
cider vinegar

der
**Gewürzessig**
balsamic vinegar

die **Flasche**
bottle

**der Ketchup**
ketchup

**der englische
Senf**
English mustard

**die Majonäse**
mayonnaise

**das Chutney**
chutney

**der Malzessig**
malt vinegar

**der Weinessig**
wine vinegar

**der Essig**
vinegar

**die Soße**
sauce

**der französische
Senf**
French mustard

**der grobe Senf**
whole-grain
mustard

---

**das Einmachglas**
canning jar

**die
Erdnussbutter**
peanut butter

**der
Schokoladenaufstrich**
chocolate spread

**das eingemachte
Obst**
preserved fruit

**Vokabular •** vocabulary

**das Pflanzenöl**
vegetable oil

**das Rapsöl**
canola oil

**das
Maiskeimöl**
corn oil

**das
kaltgepresste Öl**
cold-pressed oil

**das Erdnussöl**
peanut oil

# die Milchprodukte • dairy products

## der Käse • cheese

**der geriebene Käse**
grated cheese

**der mittelharte Käse**
semi-hard cheese

**die Rinde**
rind

**der Hartkäse**
hard cheese

**der halbfeste Käse**
semi-soft cheese

**der Hüttenkäse**
cottage cheese

**der Rahmkäse**
cream cheese

**der Blauschimmelkäse**
blue cheese

**der Weichkäse**
soft cheese

**der Frischkäse** | fresh cheese

## die Milch • milk

**die Vollmilch**
whole milk

**die Halbfettmilch**
reduced-fat milk

**die Magermilch**
skim milk

**die Milchtüte**
milk carton

**die Ziegenmilch**
goat's milk

**die Kondensmilch**
condensed milk

**die Kuhmilch** | cow's milk

**die Butter**
butter

**die Margarine**
margarine

**die Sahne**
cream

**die fettarme Sahne**
half-and-half

**die Schlagsahne**
heavy cream

**die Schlagsahne**
whipped cream

**die saure Sahne**
sour cream

**der Joghurt**
yogurt

**das Eis**
ice cream

# die Eier • eggs

**das Eigelb**
yolk

**das Eiweiß**
egg white

**die Eierschale**
shell

**der Eier becher**
eggcup

**das gekochte Ei**
soft-boiled egg

**das Hühnerei**
hen's egg

**das Entenei**
duck egg

**das Gänseei**
goose egg

**das Wachtelei**
quail egg

## Vokabular • vocabulary

| | | | | | |
|---|---|---|---|---|---|
| **pasteurisiert**<br>pasteurized | **fettfrei**<br>fat-free | **gesalzen**<br>salted | **die Schafmilch**<br>sheep's milk | **die Laktose**<br>lactose | **der Milchshake**<br>milk shake |
| **unpasteurisiert**<br>unpasteurized | **das Milchpulver**<br>powdered milk | **ungesalzen**<br>unsalted | **die Buttermilch**<br>buttermilk | **homogenisiert**<br>homogenized | **der gefrorene Joghurt**<br>frozen yogurt |

# das Brot und das Mehl • breads and flours

**das Scheibenbrot**
sliced bread

**der Mohn**
poppy seeds

**das Roggenbrot**
rye bread

**das Baguette**
baguette

**die Bäckerei** | bakery

## Brot backen • making bread

**das Weizenmehl**
white flour

**das Roggenmehl**
brown flour

**das Vollkornmehl**
whole-wheat flour

**die Hefe**
yeast

**sieben** | sift (v)

**verrühren** | mix (v)

**der Teig**
dough

**Kneten** | knead (v)

**backen** | bake (v)

**deutsch** • english

**die Kruste**
crust

**der Laib**
loaf

**die Scheibe**
slice

**das Weißbrot**
white bread

**das Graubrot**
brown bread

**das Vollkornbrot**
whole-wheat bread

**das Mehrkornbrot**
multigrain bread

**das Maisbrot**
corn bread

**das Sodabrot**
soda bread

**das Sauerteigbrot**
sourdough bread

**das Fladenbrot**
flat bread

**der Bagel**
bagel

**das weiche Brötchen**
bun

**das Brötchen**
roll

**das Rosinenbrot**
fruit bread

**das Körnerbrot**
seeded bread

**der Naan**
naan bread

**das Pitabrot**
pita bread

**das Knäckebrot**
crispbread

## Vokabular • vocabulary

| | | | | |
|---|---|---|---|---|
| **das angereicherte Mehl**<br>bread flour | **das Paniermehl**<br>breadcrumbs | **gehen lassen**<br>prove (v) | **aufgehen**<br>rise (v) | **der Brotschneider**<br>slicer |
| **das Mehl mit Backpulver**<br>self-rising flour | **das Mehl ohne Backpulver**<br>all-purpose flour | **glasieren**<br>glaze (v) | **die Flöte**<br>flute | **der Bäcker**<br>baker |

# Kuchen und Nachspeisen • cakes and desserts

**das Eclair**
éclair

**der Brandteig**
choux pastry

**der Blätterteig**
puff pastry

**die Sahne**
cream

**der Blätterteig**
phyllo dough

**die Füllung**
filling

**der englische Kuchen**
fruitcake

**mit Schokolade überzogen**
chocolate-covered

**das Obsttortelett**
fruit tart

**der Muffin**
muffin

**das Biskuittörtchen**
sponge cake

**das Baiser**
meringue

**das Gebäck** | cakes

## Vokabular • vocabulary

| | | | | |
|---|---|---|---|---|
| **die Konditorcreme**<br>crème pâtissière | **das Teilchen**<br>bun | **der Teig**<br>pastry | **der Milchreis**<br>rice pudding | **Könnte ich bitte ein Stück haben?**<br>May I have a slice, please? |
| **die Schokoladentorte**<br>chocolate cake | **der Vanillepudding**<br>custard | **das Stück**<br>slice | **die Feier**<br>celebration | |

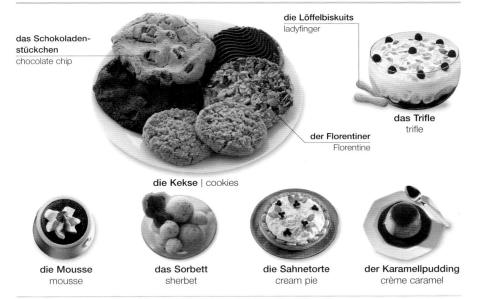

**das Schokoladen-
stückchen**
chocolate chip

**die Löffelbiskuits**
ladyfinger

**der Florentiner**
Florentine

**das Trifle**
trifle

**die Kekse** | cookies

**die Mousse**
mousse

**das Sorbett**
sherbet

**die Sahnetorte**
cream pie

**der Karamellpudding**
crème caramel

# die festlichen Kuchen • celebration cakes

**der obere Kuchenteil**
top tier

**das Band**
ribbon

**der untere
Kuchenteil**
bottom tier

**der
Zuckerguss**
frosting

**das
Marzipan**
marzipan

**die Hochzeitstorte** | wedding cake

**die
Dekoration**
decoration

**die
Geburtstagskerzen**
birthday candles

**ausblasen**
blow out (v)

**der Geburtstagskuchen** | birthday cake

# die Feinkost • delicatessen

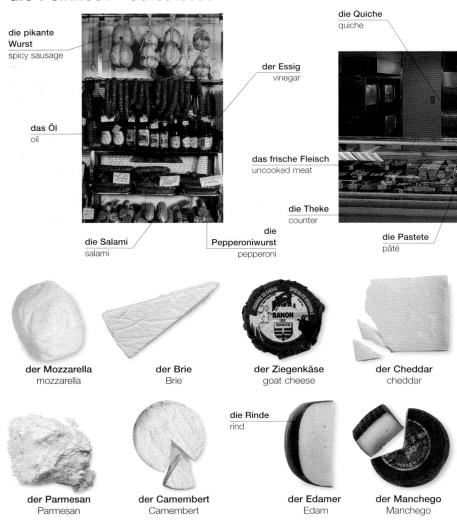

die pikante Wurst
spicy sausage

das Öl
oil

der Essig
vinegar

die Quiche
quiche

das frische Fleisch
uncooked meat

die Theke
counter

die Salami
salami

die Pepperoniwurst
pepperoni

die Pastete
pâté

der Mozzarella
mozzarella

der Brie
Brie

der Ziegenkäse
goat cheese

der Cheddar
cheddar

der Parmesan
Parmesan

der Camembert
Camembert

die Rinde
rind

der Edamer
Edam

der Manchego
Manchego

**die Pasteten**
potpie

**die schwarze Olive**
black olive

**die Peperoni**
chili pepper

**die Soße**
sauce

**das Brötchen**
bread roll

**das gekochte Fleisch**
cooked meat

**die grüne Olive**
green olive

**der Schinken**
ham

**die Sandwichtheke**
sandwich counter

**der Räucherfisch**
smoked fish

**die Kapern**
capers

**die Chorizo**
chorizo

**der Prosciutto**
prosciutto

**die gefüllte Olive**
stuffed olive

---

**Vokabular** • vocabulary

| | | |
|---|---|---|
| **in Öl**<br>in oil | **mariniert**<br>marinated | **geräuchert**<br>smoked |
| **in Lake**<br>in brine | **gepökelt**<br>salted | **getrocknet**<br>cured |

**Nehmen Sie bitte eine Nummer.**
Take a number, please.

**Kann ich bitte etwas davon probieren?**
Can I try some of that, please?

**Ich hätte gerne sechs Scheiben davon, bitte.**
May I have six slices of that, please?

---

# die Getränke • drinks

## das Wasser • water

**das Flaschenwasser**
bottled water

**mit Kohlensäure**
sparkling

**ohne Kohlensäure**
still

**das Leitungswasser**
tap water

**das Tonicwater**
tonic water

**das Mineralwasser**
mineral water

**das Sodawasser**
soda water

## die heißen Getränke • hot drinks

**der Teebeutel**
tea bag

**die Teeblätter**
loose-leaf tea

**der Tee**
tea

**die Bohnen**
beans

**der gemahlene Kaffee**
ground coffee

**der Kaffee**
coffee

**die heiße Schokolade**
hot chocolate

**das Malzgetränk**
malted drink

# die alkoholfreien Getränke • soft drinks

**der Strohhalm**
straw

**der Tomatensaft**
tomato juice

**der Traubensaft**
grape juice

**die Limonade**
lemonade

**die Orangeade**
orangeade

**die Cola**
cola

## die alkoholischen Getränke • alcoholic drinks

die Dose
can

**das Bier**
beer

**der Apfelwein**
hard cider

**das halbdunkle Bier**
bitter

**der Stout**
stout

**der Gin**
gin

**der Wodka**
vodka

**der Whisky**
whiskey

**der Rum**
rum

**der Weinbrand**
brandy

**der Portwein**
port

trocken
dry

**der Sherry**
sherry

**der Campari**
Campari

rosé
rosé

weiß
white

rot
red

**der Likör**
liqueur

**der Tequila**
tequila

**der Champagner**
champagne

**der Wein**
wine

# auswärts essen
eating out

# das Café • café

die Markise
awning

die
Speisekarte
menu

der
Sonnenschirm
umbrella

das Terrassencafé
patio café

**das Straßencafé** | sidewalk café

der
Kellner
server

die Kaffeemaschine
coffee machine

der Tisch
table

**die Snackbar** | snack bar

## der Kaffee • coffee

der Kaffee mit Milch
coffee with milk

der schwarze
Kaffee
black coffee

das
Kakaopulver
cocoa powder

der Schaum
froth

**der Filterkaffee**
filter coffee

**der Espresso**
espresso

**der Cappuccino**
cappuccino

**der Eiskaffee**
iced coffee

# der Tee • tea

der Kräutertee
herbal tea

der Kamillentee
chamomile tea

der grüne Tee
green tea

der Tee mit Milch
tea with milk

der schwarze Tee
black tea

der Tee mit
Zitrone
tea with lemon

der Pfefferminztee
mint tea

der Eistee
iced tea

# die Säfte und Milchshakes • juices and milkshakes

der
Schokoladenmilchshake
chocolate milkshake

der
Erdbeermilchshake
strawberry milkshake

der
Orangensaft
orange juice

der
Apfelsaft
apple juice

der
Ananassaft
pineapple juice

der
Tomatensaft
tomato juice

der
Kaffeemilchshake
coffee milkshake

# das Essen • food

das Graubrot
whole-wheat
bread

die Kugel
scoop

der getoastete Sandwich
toasted sandwich

der Salat
salad

das Eis
ice cream

das Gebäck
pastry

# die Bar • bar

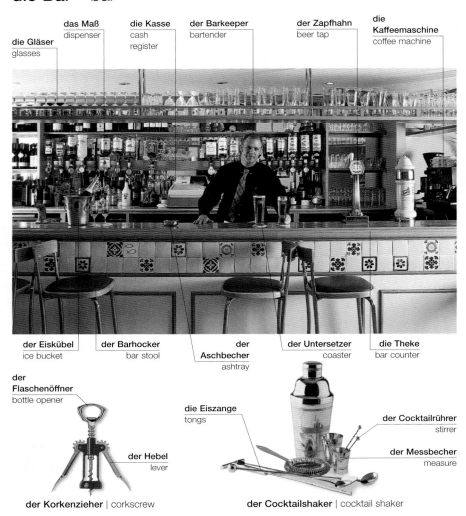

**die Gläser**
glasses

**das Maß**
dispenser

**die Kasse**
cash register

**der Barkeeper**
bartender

**der Zapfhahn**
beer tap

**die Kaffeemaschine**
coffee machine

**der Eiskübel**
ice bucket

**der Barhocker**
bar stool

**der Aschbecher**
ashtray

**der Untersetzer**
coaster

**die Theke**
bar counter

**der Flaschenöffner**
bottle opener

**der Hebel**
lever

**der Korkenzieher** | corkscrew

**die Eiszange**
tongs

**der Cocktailrührer**
stirrer

**der Messbecher**
measure

**der Cocktailshaker** | cocktail shaker

**der Krug**
pitcher

**der Eiswürfel**
ice cube

**der Gin Tonic**
gin and tonic

**der Scotch mit Wasser**
scotch and water

**der Rum mit Cola**
rum and cola

**der Wodka mit Orangensaft**
screwdriver

**der Martini**
martini

**der Cocktail**
cocktail

**der Wein**
wine

**das Bier** | beer

**einfach**
single

**doppelt**
double

**Eis und Zitrone**
ice and lemon

**ein Schnaps**
shot

**das Maß**
measure

**ohne Eis**
without ice

**mit Eis**
with ice

# die Knabbereien • bar snacks

**die Cashewnüsse**
cashews

**die Erdnüsse**
peanuts

**die Mandeln**
almonds

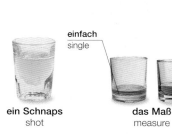

**die Kartoffelchips** | potato chips

**die Nüsse** | nuts

**die Oliven** | olives

# das Restaurant • restaurant

**das Gedeck**
table setting

**der Hilfskoch**
sous chef

**das Glas**
glass

**der Küchenchef**
chef

**das Tablett**
tray

**die Küche**
kitchen

**der Kellner**
server

---

## Vokabular • vocabulary

| | | | | | |
|---|---|---|---|---|---|
| **das Abendmenü** dinner menu | **die Spezialitäten** specials | **der Preis** price | **das Trinkgeld** tip | **das Buffet** buffet | **der Kunde** customer |
| **die Weinkarte** wine list | **à la carte** à la carte | **die Quittung** receipt | **ohne Bedienung** service charge included | **die Bar** bar | **der Pfeffer** pepper |
| **das Mittagsmenü** lunch menu | **der Dessertwagen** dessert cart | **die Rechnung** check | **Bedienung inbegriffen** service charge not included | **das Salz** salt | |

**die Speisekarte**
menu

**die Kinderportion**
child's meal

**bestellen**
order (v)

**bezahlen**
pay (v)

# die Gänge • courses

**der Aperitif**
apéritif

**die Vorspeise**
appetizer

**die Suppe**
soup

**das Hauptgericht**
entrée

**die Beilage**
side order

**der Nachtisch** | dessert

**der Kaffee** | coffee

**Ein Tisch für zwei Personen bitte.**
A table for two, please.

**Könnte ich bitte die Speisekarte/Weinliste sehen?**
Can I see the menu/wine list, please?

**Gibt es ein Festpreismenü?**
Is there a fixed-price menu?

**Haben Sie vegetarische Gerichte?**
Do you have any vegetarian dishes?

**Könnte ich die Rechnung/ Quittung haben?**
Could I have the check/a receipt, please?

**Könnten wir getrennt zahlen?**
Can we pay separately?

**Wo sind die Toiletten bitte ?**
Where is the restroom, please?

# der Schnellimbiss • fast food

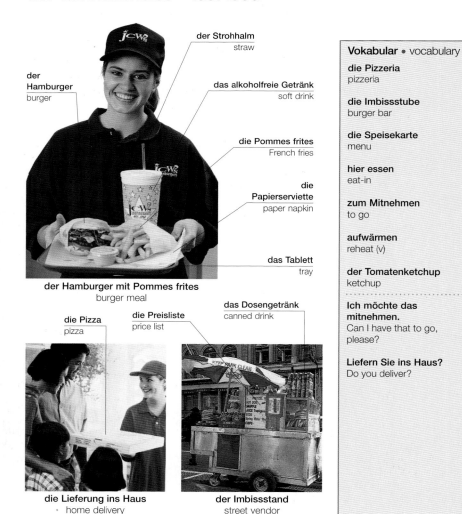

der Strohhalm
straw

der Hamburger
burger

das alkoholfreie Getränk
soft drink

die Pommes frites
French fries

die Papierserviette
paper napkin

das Tablett
tray

**der Hamburger mit Pommes frites**
burger meal

die Pizza
pizza

die Preisliste
price list

das Dosengetränk
canned drink

**die Lieferung ins Haus**
· home delivery

**der Imbissstand**
street vendor

**Vokabular** • vocabulary

**die Pizzeria**
pizzeria

**die Imbissstube**
burger bar

**die Speisekarte**
menu

**hier essen**
eat-in

**zum Mitnehmen**
to go

**aufwärmen**
reheat (v)

**der Tomatenketchup**
ketchup

**Ich möchte das mitnehmen.**
Can I have that to go, please?

**Liefern Sie ins Haus?**
Do you deliver?

**der Hamburger**
hamburger

**der Chickenburger**
chicken burger

das **Brötchen**
bun

**der vegetarische Hamburger**
veggie burger

der **Senf**
mustard

die **Wurst**
sausage

**das Hot Dog**
hot dog

**der Sandwich**
sandwich

**der Klubsandwich**
club sandwich

**das belegte Brot**
open-faced sandwich

die **Füllung**
filling

**der Wrap**
wrap

die **Soße**
sauce

salzig
savory

süß
sweet

**der Kebab**
kebab

**die Hähnchenstückchen**
chicken nuggets

**die Crêpes** | crêpes

der **Pizzabelag**
topping

**der Bratfisch mit Pommes frites**
fish and chips

**die Rippen**
ribs

**das gebratene Hähnchen**
fried chicken

**die Pizza**
pizza

# das Frühstück • breakfast

die **Milch** | milk

die **Getreide flocken** | cereal

die **Konfitüre** | jam

das **Dörrobst** | dried fruit

der **Schinken** | ham

der **Käse** | cheese

das **Knäckebrot** | crispbread

**das Frühstücksbuffet** | breakfast buffet

die **Orangenmarmelade** | marmalade

die **Pastete** | pâté

die **Butter** | butter

der **Obstsaft** | fruit juice

der **Kaffee** | coffee

die **Schokolade** | hot chocolate

das **Croissant** | croissant

der **Tee** | tea

**der Frühstückstisch** | breakfast table

**die Getränke** | drinks

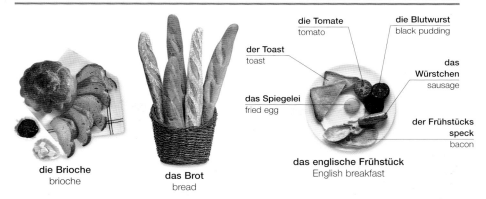

die Tomate
tomato

die Blutwurst
black pudding

der Toast
toast

das
Würstchen
sausage

das Spiegelei
fried egg

der Frühstücks
speck
bacon

**das englische Frühstück**
English breakfast

**die Brioche**
brioche

**das Brot**
bread

die Räucherheringe
kippers

**die Armen Ritter**
French toast

das Eigelb
yolk

**das gekochte Ei**
soft-boiled egg

**das Rührei**
scrambled eggs

die Sahne
whipped cream

der Früchtejoghurt
fruit yogurt

**die Pfannkuchen**
crepes

**die Waffeln**
waffles

**der Porridge**
oatmeal

**das Obst**
fresh fruit

# die Hauptmahlzeit • dinner

**die Suppe** | soup

**die Brühe** | broth

**der Eintopf** | stew

**das Curry** | curry

**der Braten**
roast

**die Pastete**
potpie

**das Soufflé**
soufflé

**der Schaschlik**
kebab

**die Fleischklöße**
meatballs

**das Omelett**
omelet

**das Schnellbratgericht**
stir-fry

**die Nudeln**
noodles

**die Nudeln** | pasta

**der Reis**
rice

**der gemischte Salat**
tossed salad

**der grüne Salat**
green salad

**die Salatsoße**
dressing

# die Zubereitung • techniques

**gefüllt** | stuffed

**in Soße** | in sauce

**gegrillt** | grilled

**mariniert** | marinated

**pochiert** | poached

**püriert** | mashed

**gebacken** | baked

**kurzgebraten** | pan-fried

**gebraten**
fried

**eingelegt**
pickled

**geräuchert**
smoked

**frittiert**
deep-fried

**in Saft**
in syrup

**angemacht**
dressed

**gedämpft**
steamed

**getrocknet**
cured

**das Lernen**
study

# die Schule • school

**die Weißwandtafel**
whiteboard

**die Lehrerin**
teacher

**die Schultasche**
schoolbag

**der Schüler**
student

**das Pult**
desk

**das Klassenzimmer** | classroom

**das Schulmädchen**
schoolgirl

**der Schuljunge**
schoolboy

| Vokabular • vocabulary | | |
|---|---|---|
| **die Literatur**<br>literature | **die Kunst**<br>art | **die Physik**<br>physics |
| **die Sprachen**<br>languages | **die Musik**<br>music | **die Chemie**<br>chemistry |
| **die Erdkunde**<br>geography | **die Mathematik**<br>math | **die Biologie**<br>biology |
| **die Geschichte**<br>history | **die Naturwissenschaft**<br>science | **der Sport**<br>physical education |

## die Aktivitäten • activities

**lesen** | read (v)

**schreiben** | write (v)

**buchstabieren**
spell (v)

**zeichnen**
draw (v)

**die Feder**
nib

**der Buntstift**
colored pencil

**der Anspitzer**
pencil
sharpener

**der Digitalprojektor**
digital projector

**der Füller**
pen

**der Bleistift**
pencil

**der Radiergummi**
eraser

**das Heft**
notebook

**das Federmäppchen**
pencil case

**das Lineal**
ruler

**das Schulbuch** | textbook

**fragen**
question (v)

**antworten**
answer (v)

**diskutieren**
discuss (v)

**lernen**
learn (v)

| **Vokabular** • vocabulary | | |
|---|---|---|
| **der Schulleiter** principal | **die Antwort** answer | **die Note** grade |
| **die Stunde** lesson | **der Aufsatz** essay | **die Klasse** year |
| **die Frage** question | **die Prüfung** test | **das Lexikon** encyclopedia |
| **Notizen machen** take notes (v) | **die Hausaufgabe** homework | **das Wörterbuch** dictionary |

# die Mathematik • math

## die Formen • shapes

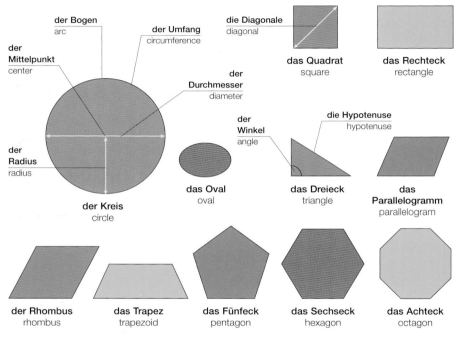

der Bogen
arc

der Umfang
circumference

die Diagonale
diagonal

der
Mittelpunkt
center

der
Durchmesser
diameter

das Quadrat
square

das Rechteck
rectangle

der
Radius
radius

der
Winkel
angle

die Hypotenuse
hypotenuse

das Oval
oval

der Kreis
circle

das Dreieck
triangle

das
Parallelogramm
parallelogram

der Rhombus
rhombus

das Trapez
trapezoid

das Fünfeck
pentagon

das Sechseck
hexagon

das Achteck
octagon

## die Körper • solids

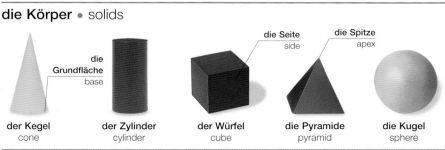

die
Grundfläche
base

die Seite
side

die Spitze
apex

der Kegel
cone

der Zylinder
cylinder

der Würfel
cube

die Pyramide
pyramid

die Kugel
sphere

# die Linien • lines

**gerade**
straight

**parallel**
parallel

**senkrecht**
perpendicular

**gekrümmt**
curved

# die Maße • measurements

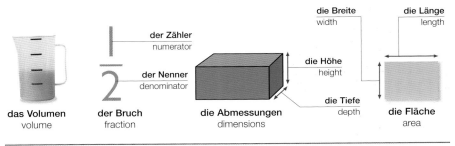

**das Volumen**
volume

**der Bruch**
fraction

der Zähler
numerator

der Nenner
denominator

**die Abmessungen**
dimensions

die Breite
width

die Höhe
height

die Tiefe
depth

die Länge
length

**die Fläche**
area

# die Ausrüstung • equipment

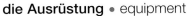

**das Zeichendreieck**
triangle

**der Winkelmesser**
protractor

**das Lineal**
ruler

**der Zirkel**
compass

**der Taschenrechner**
calculator

| **Vokabular** • vocabulary | | | | | | |
|---|---|---|---|---|---|---|
| **die Geometrie** geometry | **plus** plus | **mal** times | **gleich** equals | **addieren** add (v) | **multiplizieren** multiply (v) | **die Gleichung** equation |
| **die Arithmetik** arithmetic | **minus** minus | **geteilt durch** divided by | **zählen** count (v) | **subtrahieren** subtract (v) | **dividieren** divide (v) | **der Prozentsatz** percentage |

# die Wissenschaft • science

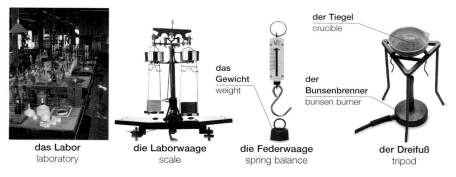

**das Labor**
laboratory

**die Laborwaage**
scale

**das Gewicht**
weight

**die Federwaage**
spring balance

**der Tiegel**
crucible

**der Bunsenbrenner**
bunsen burner

**der Dreifuß**
tripod

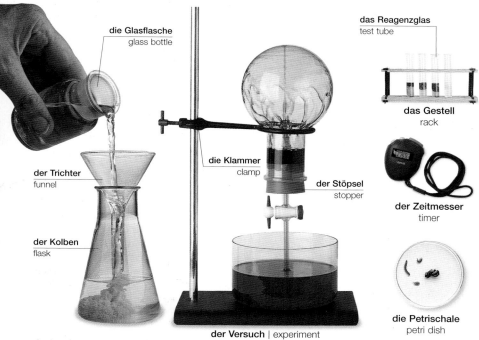

**die Glasflasche**
glass bottle

**das Reagenzglas**
test tube

**das Gestell**
rack

**der Trichter**
funnel

**die Klammer**
clamp

**der Stöpsel**
stopper

**der Zeitmesser**
timer

**der Kolben**
flask

**die Petrischale**
petri dish

**der Versuch** | experiment

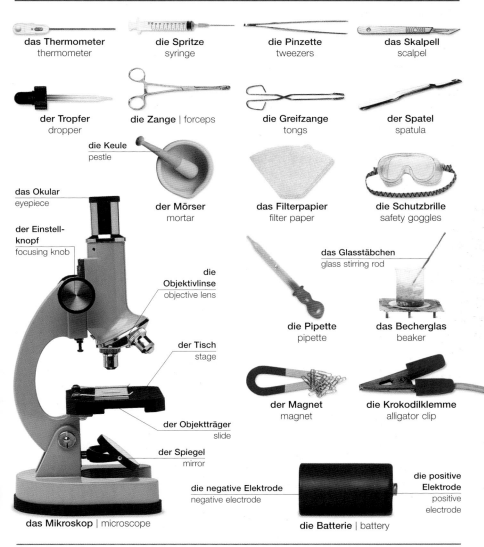

**das Thermometer**
thermometer

**die Spritze**
syringe

**die Pinzette**
tweezers

**das Skalpell**
scalpel

**der Tropfer**
dropper

**die Zange** | forceps

**die Greifzange**
tongs

**der Spatel**
spatula

**die Keule**
pestle

**der Mörser**
mortar

**das Filterpapier**
filter paper

**die Schutzbrille**
safety goggles

**das Okular**
eyepiece

**der Einstell-knopf**
focusing knob

**die Objektivlinse**
objective lens

**das Glasstäbchen**
glass stirring rod

**die Pipette**
pipette

**das Becherglas**
beaker

**der Tisch**
stage

**der Magnet**
magnet

**die Krokodilklemme**
alligator clip

**der Objektträger**
slide

**der Spiegel**
mirror

**die negative Elektrode**
negative electrode

**die positive Elektrode**
positive electrode

**das Mikroskop** | microscope

**die Batterie** | battery

# die Hochschule • college

**das Sekretariat**
admissions office

**die Mensa**
cafeteria

**die Gesundheits-
fürsorge**
health center

**der
Sportplatz**
playing field

**das
Studenten-
wohnheim**
residence hall

**der Campus** | campus

**Vokabular** • vocabulary

| | | |
|---|---|---|
| **der Leserausweis** library card | **die Auskunft** help desk | **verlängern** renew (v) |
| **der Lesesaal** reading room | **ausleihen** borrow (v) | **das Buch** book |
| **die Literaturliste** reading list | **vorbestellen** reserve (v) | **der Titel** title |
| **das Rückgabedatum** due date | **die Ausleihe** loan | **der Gang** aisle |

**die Bibliothekarin**
librarian

**die Ausleihe**
circulation desk

**das Bücher
regal**
bookshelf

**das
Periodikum**
periodical

**die
Zeitschrift**
journal

**die Bibliothek** | library

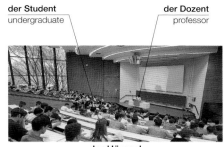

der Student — undergraduate

der Dozent — professor

**der Hörsaal**
lecture hall

die Graduierte — graduate

die Robe — gown

**die Graduierungsfeier**
graduation ceremony

# die Fachhochschulen • schools

das Model — model

**die Kunsthochschule**
art school

**die Musikhochschule**
music school

**die Tanzakademie**
dance school

## Vokabular • vocabulary

| | | | | |
|---|---|---|---|---|
| **das Stipendium** scholarship | **die Forschung** research | **die Examensarbeit** dissertation | **die Medizin** medicine | **die Philosophie** philosophy |
| **postgraduiert** postgraduate | **der Magister** master's | **der Fachbereich** department | **die Zoologie** zoology | **die Politologie** political science |
| **das Diplom** diploma | **die Promotion** doctorate | **der Maschinenbau** engineering | **die Physik** physics | **die Literatur** literature |
| **der akademische Grad** degree | **die Dissertation** thesis | **die Kunstgeschichte** art history | **die Rechtswissenschaft** law | |
| | | | **die Wirtschaftswissenschaft** economics | |

**die Arbeit**
work

# das Büro 1 • office 1

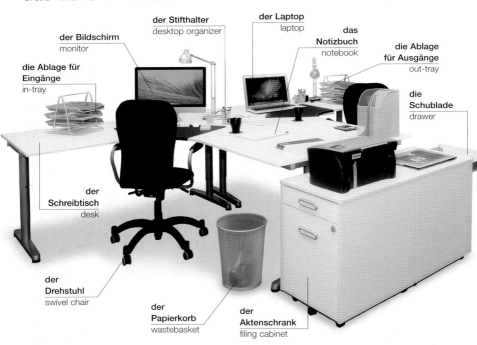

der Stifthalter
desktop organizer

der Laptop
laptop

das Notizbuch
notebook

der Bildschirm
monitor

die Ablage für Eingänge
in-tray

die Ablage für Ausgänge
out-tray

die Schublade
drawer

der Schreibtisch
desk

der Drehstuhl
swivel chair

der Papierkorb
wastebasket

der Aktenschrank
filing cabinet

## die Büroausstattung • office equipment

der Papierbehälter
paper tray

der Drucker | printer

der Aktenvernichter | shredder

| Vokabular • vocabulary | |
|---|---|
| drucken print (v) | vergrößern enlarge (v) |
| kopieren copy (v) | verkleinern reduce (v) |

**Ich möchte fotokopieren.**
I need to make some copies.

# der Bürobedarf • office supplies

der Empfehlungszettel
compliments slip

der Geschäftsbogen
letterhead

der Briefumschlag
envelope

der Aktenordner
box file

der Kartenreiter
tab

der Teiler
divider

das Klemmbrett
clipboard

der Notizblock
notepad

der Hängeordner
hanging file

der Fächerordner
expanding file

der Leitz-Ordner
binder

die Klammern
staples

der Tesafilm
tape

das Stempelkissen
ink pad

der Terminkalender
personal organizer

der Hefter
stapler

der Tesafilmhalter
tape dispenser

der Locher
hole punch

der Stempel
rubber stamp

der Reißnagel
thumbtack

das Gummiband
rubber band

die Papierklammer
bulldog clip

die Büroklammer
paper clip

die Pinnward | bulletin board

# das Büro 2 • office 2

**das Flipchart**
flip chart

**das Gestell**
easel

**das Protokoll**
minutes

**der Bericht**
report

**der Manager**
manager

**das Angebot**
proposal

**der leitende Angestellte**
executive

**die Sitzung** | meeting

**Vokabular** • vocabulary

| | |
|---|---|
| **der Sitzungsraum**<br>meeting room | **teilnehmen**<br>attend (v) |
| **die Tagesordnung**<br>agenda | **den Vorsitz führen**<br>chair (v) |

**Um wieviel Uhr ist die Sitzung?**
What time is the meeting?

**Was sind Ihre Geschäftszeiten?**
What are your office hours?

**der Sprecher**
speaker

**die Präsentation** | presentation

# das Geschäft • business

**der Geschäftsmann**
businessman

**die Geschäftsfrau**
businesswoman

**das Arbeitsessen**
business lunch

**die Geschäftsreise**
business trip

**der Termin**
appointment

**der**
**Geschäftsführer**
CEO

**der Kunde**
client

**der Terminkalender** | day planner

**das Geschäftsabkommen**
business deal

## Vokabular • vocabulary

| | | | |
|---|---|---|---|
| **die Firma**<br>company | **das Personal**<br>staff | **die Buchhaltung**<br>accounting department | **die Rechtsabteilung**<br>legal department |
| **die Zentrale**<br>head office | **die Lohnliste**<br>payroll | **die Marketingabteilung**<br>marketing department | **die Kundendienstabteilung**<br>customer service department |
| **die Zweigstelle**<br>regional office | **das Gehalt**<br>salary | **die Verkaufsabteilung**<br>sales department | **die Personalabteilung**<br>human resources department |

# der Computer • computer

**der Drucker**
printer

**der Bildschirm**
screen

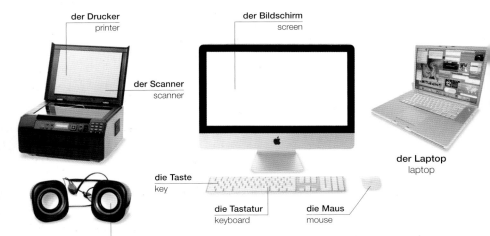

**der Scanner**
scanner

**der Laptop**
laptop

**die Taste**
key

**die Tastatur**
keyboard

**die Maus**
mouse

**der Lautsprecher**
speaker

**die Hardware**
hardware

**der Memorystick**
memory stick

**die externe Festplatte**
external hard drive

| **Vokabular** • vocabulary | | |
|---|---|---|
| **das RAM**<br>RAM | **die Software**<br>software | **der Server**<br>server |
| **die Bytes**<br>bytes | **das Programm**<br>program | **der Port**<br>port |
| **das System**<br>system | **das Netzwerk**<br>network | **der Prozessor**<br>processor |
| **der Speicher**<br>memory | **die Anwendung**<br>application | **das Stromkabel**<br>power cord |

**das Tablet**
tablet

**das Smartphone**
smartphone

# das Desktop • desktop

**der Menübalken**
menubar

**die Werkzeugleiste**
toolbar

**der Bildschirmhintergrund**
wallpaper

**die Schriftart**
font

**das Symbol**
icon

**der Scrollbalken**
scrollbar

**das Fenster**
window

**die Datei**
file

**der Ordner**
folder

**der Papierkorb**
trash

---

# das Internet • internet

**der Browser**
browser

**browsen**
browse (v)

**der Posteingang**
inbox

**die Webseite**
website

# die E-Mail • email

**die E-Mail-Adresse**
email address

---

**Vokabular** • vocabulary

| | | | | | |
|---|---|---|---|---|---|
| **verbinden** connect (v) | **der Serviceprovider** service provider | **einloggen** log on (v) | **herunterladen** download (v) | **senden** send (v) | **sichern** save (v) |
| **installieren** install (v) | **das E-Mail-Konto** email account | **online** online | **der Anhang** attachment | **erhalten** receive (v) | **suchen** search (v) |

---

# die Medien • media

## das Fernsehstudio • television studio

die
**Studioeinrichtung**
set

der
**Moderator**
host

die
**Beleuchtung**
light

die **Kamera**
camera

der **Kamerakran**
camera crane

der **Kameramann**
cameraman

---

**Vokabular** • vocabulary

| | | | | | |
|---|---|---|---|---|---|
| **der Kanal**<br>channel | **die Nachrichten**<br>news | **die Presse**<br>press | **senden**<br>broadcast (v) | **live**<br>live | **der Zeichentrickfilm**<br>cartoon |
| **die Programm–<br>gestaltung**<br>programming | **der<br>Dokumentarfilm**<br>documentary | **die<br>Fernsehserie**<br>television series | **die<br>Spielshow**<br>game show | **vorher<br>aufgezeichnet**<br>prerecorded | **die<br>Seifenoper**<br>soap opera |

---

**der Interviewer**
interviewer

**die Reporterin**
reporter

**der Teleprompter**
teleprompter

**die Nachrichtensprecherin**
anchor

**die Schauspieler**
actors

**der Mikrophongalgen**
sound boom

**die Klappe**
clapper board

**das Set**
movie set

## das Radio • radio

**der Tonmeister**
sound technician

**das Mischpult**
mixing desk

**das Mikrophon**
microphone

**das Tonstudio** | recording studio

**Vokabular • vocabulary**

| | |
|---|---|
| **der DJ** DJ | **die Kurzwelle** short wave |
| **die Sendung** broadcast | **die Mittelwelle** medium wave |
| **die Wellenlänge** wavelength | **die Frequenz** frequency |
| **die Langwelle** long wave | **die Lautstärke** volume |
| **die Rundfunkstation** radio station | **einstellen** tune (v) |
| **digital** digital | **analog** analog |

# das Recht • law

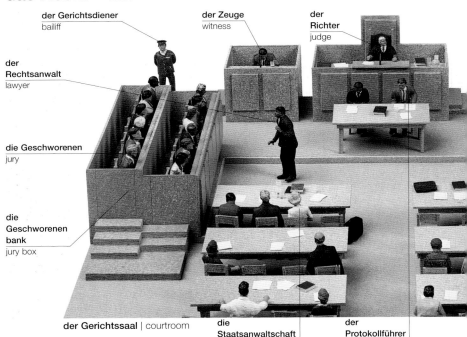

der Gerichtsdiener
bailiff

der Zeuge
witness

der Richter
judge

der Rechtsanwalt
lawyer

die Geschworenen
jury

die Geschworenen bank
jury box

der Gerichtssaal | courtroom

die Staatsanwaltschaft
prosecution

der Protokollführer
court clerk

## Vokabular • vocabulary

| | | | |
|---|---|---|---|
| **das Anwaltsbüro** lawyer's office | **die Vorladung** summons | **die Verfügung** writ | **das Gerichtsverfahren** court case |
| **die Rechtsberatung** legal advice | **die Aussage** statement | **der Gerichtstermin** court date | **die Anklage** charge |
| **der Klient** client | **der Haftbefehl** warrant | **das Plädoyer** plea | **der Angeklagte** accused |

**der Gerichtsstenograf**
stenographer

**der Verdächtige**
suspect

**der Angeklagte**
defendant

**die Verteidigung**
defense

**das Phantombild**
composite sketch

**der Straftäter**
criminal

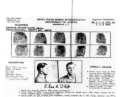

**das Strafregister**
criminal record

**der Gefängniswärter**
prison guard

**die Gefängniszelle**
cell

**das Gefängnis**
prison

---

**Vokabular** • vocabulary

| | | | |
|---|---|---|---|
| **das Beweismittel**<br>evidence | **schuldig**<br>guilty | **die Kaution**<br>bail | **Ich möchte mit einem Anwalt sprechen.**<br>I want to see a lawyer. |
| **das Urteil**<br>verdict | **freigesprochen**<br>acquitted | **die Berufung**<br>appeal | **Wo ist das Gericht?**<br>Where is the courthouse? |
| **unschuldig**<br>innocent | **das Strafmaß**<br>sentence | **die Haftentlassung auf Bewährung**<br>parole | **Kann ich die Kaution leisten?**<br>Can I post bail? |

---

# der Bauernhof 1 • farm 1

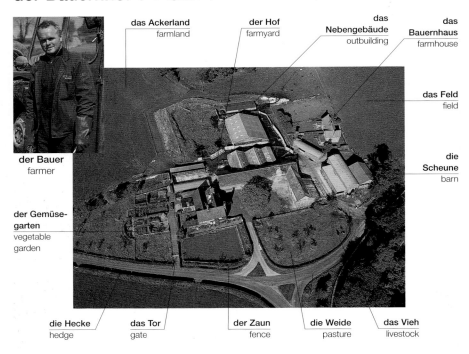

**das Ackerland**
farmland

**der Hof**
farmyard

**das Nebengebäude**
outbuilding

**das Bauernhaus**
farmhouse

**das Feld**
field

**die Scheune**
barn

**der Bauer**
farmer

**der Gemüse-garten**
vegetable garden

**die Hecke**
hedge

**das Tor**
gate

**der Zaun**
fence

**die Weide**
pasture

**das Vieh**
livestock

**der Kultivator**
cultivator

**der Traktor** | tractor

**der Mähdrescher** | combine

# die landwirtschaftlichen Betriebe • types of farms

**die Feldfrucht**
crop

**die Herde**
flock

**der Ackerbaubetrieb**
crop farm

**der Betrieb für Milchproduktion**
dairy farm

**die Schaffarm**
sheep farm

**die Hühnerfarm**
poultry farm

**der Weinstock**
vine

**die Schweinefarm**
pig farm

**die Fischzucht**
fish farm

**der Obstanbau**
fruit farm

**der Weinberg**
vineyard

# die Tätigkeiten • actions

**die Furche**
furrow

**pflügen**
plow (v)

**säen**
sow (v)

**melken**
milk (v)

**füttern**
feed (v)

**bewässern** | water (v)

**ernten** | harvest (v)

| **Vokabular** • vocabulary | | |
|---|---|---|
| **das Herbizid** herbicide | **die Herde** herd | **der Trog** trough |
| **das Pestizid** pesticide | **der Silo** silo | **pflanzen** plant (v) |

# der Bauernhof 2 • farm 2

## die Feldfrüchte • crops

**der Weizen**
wheat

**der Mais**
corn

**die Gerste**
barley

**der Raps**
rapeseed

**die Sonnenblume**
sunflower

der Ballen
bale

**das Heu**
hay

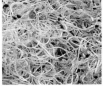

**die Luzerne**
alfalfa

**der Tabak**
tobacco

**der Reis**
rice

**der Tee**
tea

**der Kaffee**
coffee

**der Flachs**
flax

**das Zuckerrohr**
sugarcane

**die Baumwolle**
cotton

**die Vogelscheuche**
scarecrow

# das Vieh • livestock

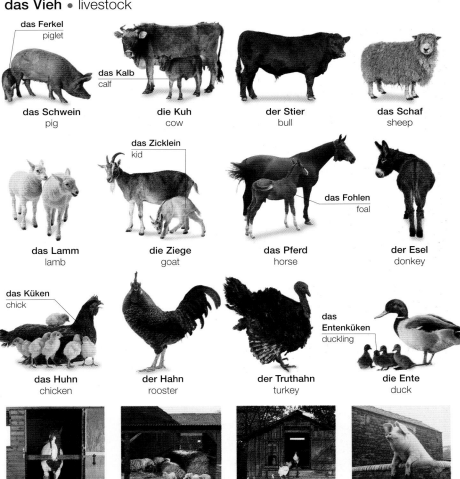

**das Ferkel**
piglet

**das Kalb**
calf

**das Schwein**
pig

**die Kuh**
cow

**der Stier**
bull

**das Schaf**
sheep

**das Zicklein**
kid

**das Fohlen**
foal

**das Lamm**
lamb

**die Ziege**
goat

**das Pferd**
horse

**der Esel**
donkey

**das Küken**
chick

**das
Entenküken**
duckling

**das Huhn**
chicken

**der Hahn**
rooster

**der Truthahn**
turkey

**die Ente**
duck

**der Stall**
stable

**der Pferch**
pen

**der Hühnerstall**
chicken coop

**der Schweinestall**
pigsty

# der Bau • construction

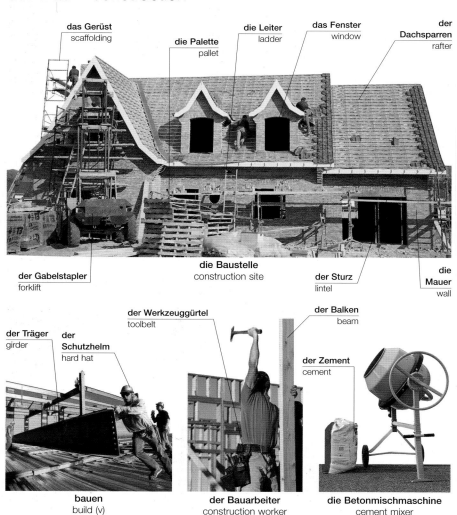

das Gerüst
scaffolding

die Palette
pallet

die Leiter
ladder

das Fenster
window

der
Dachsparren
rafter

der Gabelstapler
forklift

die Baustelle
construction site

der Sturz
lintel

die
Mauer
wall

der Werkzeuggürtel
toolbelt

der Balken
beam

der Träger
girder

der
Schutzhelm
hard hat

der Zement
cement

bauen
build (v)

der Bauarbeiter
construction worker

die Betonmischmaschine
cement mixer

# das Material • materials

**der Ziegelstein**
brick

**das Bauholz**
lumber

**der Dachziegel**
roof tile

**der Baustein**
cinder block

# die Werkzeuge • tools

**der Mörtel**
mortar

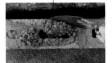

**die Kelle**
trowel

**die Wasserwaage**
level

**der Stiel**
handle

**der Vorschlaghammer**
sledgehammer

**die Spitzhacke**
pickax

**die Schaufel**
shovel

# die Maschinen • machinery

**die Walze**
road roller

**der Kipper**
dump truck

**die Stütze**
support

**der Haken**
hook

**der Kran** | crane

# die Straßenarbeiten • roadwork

**der Asphalt**
asphalt

**der Leitkegel**
cone

**der Pressluftbohrer**
jackhammer

**der Neubelag**
resurfacing

**der Bagger**
excavator

# die Berufe 1 • occupations 1

**der Schreiner**
carpenter

**der Elektriker**
electrician

**der Klempner**
plumber

**der Maurer**
construction worker

**der Gärtner**
gardener

**der Staubsauger**
vacuum cleaner

**der Gebäudereiniger**
cleaner

**der Mechaniker**
mechanic

**der Metzger**
butcher

**der Friseur**
hairdresser

**die Fischhändlerin**
fish seller

**der Gemüsehändler**
produce seller

**die Floristin**
florist

**der Friseur**
barber

**der Juwelier**
jeweler

**die Verkäuferin**
salesperson

**die Immobilienmaklerin**
realtor

**der Optiker**
optometrist

die Maske
mask

**die Zahnärztin**
dentist

**der Arzt**
doctor

**die Apothekerin**
pharmacist

**die Krankenschwester**
nurse

**die Tierärztin**
veterinarian

**der Landwirt**
farmer

**der Fischer**
fisherman

das Abzeichen
badge

die Uniform
uniform

**der Wächter**
security guard

das
Maschinen-
gewehr
machine
gun

**der Seemann**
sailor

**der Soldat**
soldier

**der Polizist**
police officer

**der Feuerwehrmann**
firefighter

# die Berufe 2 • occupations 2

das Modell
model

**die Rechtsanwältin**
lawyer

**der Wirtschaftsprüfer**
accountant

**der Architekt**
architect

**die Wissenschaftlerin**
scientist

**die Lehrerin**
teacher

**der Bibliothekar**
librarian

**die Empfangsdame**
receptionist

die
Posttasche
mailbag

**der Briefträger**
mail carrier

**der Busfahrer**
bus driver

**der Lastwagenfahrer**
truck driver

**der Taxifahrer**
taxi driver

**der Pilot**
pilot

**die Flugbegleiterin**
flight attendant

**die Reisebürokauffrau**
travel agent

die
Kochmütze
chef's hat

**der Koch**
chef

das
Ballett
röckchen
tutu

**der Musiker**
musician

**die Tänzerin**
dancer

**die Schauspielerin**
actress

**die Sängerin**
singer

**die Kellnerin**
waitress

**der Barkeeper**
bartender

**der Sportler**
sportsman

**der Bildhauer**
sculptor

**die Malerin**
painter

**der Fotograf**
photographer

**die Nachrichtensprecherin**
anchor

die Notizen
notes

**der Journalist**
journalist

**die Redakteurin**
editor

**der Designer**
designer

**die Damenschneiderin**
seamstress

**der Schneider**
tailor

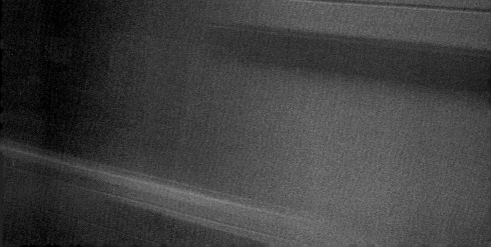

**der Verkehr**
transportation

# die Straßen • roads

die Autobahn
freeway

die Mautstelle
toll booth

die Straßen-
markierungen
road markings

die
Zufahrtsstraße
on-ramp

Einbahn-
one-way

die Verkehrsinsel
divider

die Kreuzung
interchange

die
Verkehrs-
ampel
traffic light

der
Lastwagen
truck

die rechte Spur
right lane

die mittlere Spur
middle lane

die Überholspur
left lane

die Ausfahrt
off-ramp

der Verkehr
traffic

die
Überführung
overpass

der Seitenstreifen
shoulder

der Mittelstreifen
median strip

die Unterführung
underpass

**die Notrufsäule**
emergency phone

**der Behindertenparkplatz**
disabled parking

**der Fußgängerüberweg**
crosswalk

**der Verkehrsstau**
traffic jam

**das Navi**
satnav

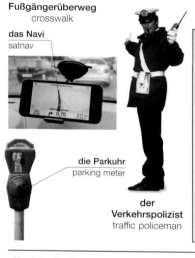

**die Parkuhr**
parking meter

**der Verkehrspolizist**
traffic policeman

**Vokabular** • vocabulary

| | | |
|---|---|---|
| **parken**<br>park (v) | **die Umleitung**<br>detour | **der Kreisverkehr**<br>roundabout |
| **überholen**<br>pass (v) | **die Leitplanke**<br>guardrail | **Ist dies die Straße nach...?**<br>Is this the road to...? |
| **rückwärts fahren**<br>reverse (v) | **die Straßenbaustelle**<br>roadwork | **Wo kann ich parken?**<br>Where can I park? |
| **fahren**<br>drive (v) | **die Schnellstraße**<br>divided highway | |
| **die abschleppen**<br>tow away (v) | | |

## die Verkehrsschilder • road signs

**keine Einfahrt**
do not enter

**die Geschwindig-keitsbegrenzung**
speed limit

**Gefahr**
hazard

**Halten verboten**
no stopping

**rechts abbiegen verboten**
no right turn

# der Bus • bus

der **Fahrersitz**
driver's seat

der **Haltegriff**
handrail

die **Automatiktür**
automatic door

das **Vorderrad**
front wheel

das **Gepäckfach**
luggage hold

**die Tür** | door

**der Reisebus** | long-distance bus

## die Bustypen • types of buses

die **Liniennummer**
route number

der **Fahrer**
driver

**der Doppeldecker**
double-decker bus

**die Straßenbahn**
tram

der **Obus**
streetcar

**der Schulbus** | school bus

**das Hinterrad**
rear wheel

**das Fenster**
window

**der Halteknopf**
stop button

**der Fahrschein**
bus ticket

**die Klingel**
bell

**der Busbahnhof**
bus station

**die
Bushaltestelle**
bus stop

**Vokabular** • vocabulary

| | |
|---|---|
| **der Fahrpreis**<br>fare | **der Rollstuhlzugang**<br>wheelchair access |
| **der Fahrplan**<br>schedule | **das Wartehäuschen**<br>bus shelter |
| Halten Sie am…?<br>Do you stop at…? | Welcher Bus fährt nach…?<br>Which bus goes to…? |

**der Kleinbus**
minibus

AIRPORT EXPRESS
VIA CENTRAL RAILWAY & DOMESTIC TERMINALS

300 **CITY**

**AIRPORT EXPRESS**

**der Zubringer** | shuttle bus

This is an official London Sightseeing Bus.

LONDON PRIDE

**der Touristenbus** | tour bus

# das Auto 1 • car 1

## das Äußere • exterior

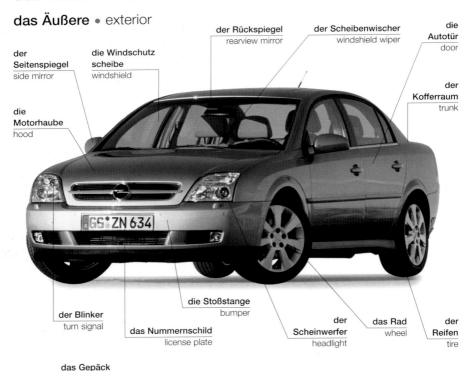

der Rückspiegel
rearview mirror

der Scheibenwischer
windshield wiper

die Autotür
door

der Seitenspiegel
side mirror

die Windschutzscheibe
windshield

der Kofferraum
trunk

die Motorhaube
hood

der Blinker
turn signal

die Stoßstange
bumper

das Nummernschild
license plate

der Scheinwerfer
headlight

das Rad
wheel

der Reifen
tire

das Gepäck
luggage

**der Dachgepäckträger**
roof rack

**die Hecktür**
tailgate

**der Sicherheitsgurt**
seat belt

**der Kindersitz**
car seat

# die Wagentypen • types

**das Elektroauto**
electric car

**die Fließhecklimousine**
hatchback

**die Limousine**
sedan

**der Kombiwagen**
station wagon

**das Kabriolett**
convertible

**das Sportkabriolett**
sports car

**die Großraum-
limousine**
minivan

**der Geländewagen**
four-wheel drive

**das Vorkriegsmodell**
vintage

**die verlängerte Limousine**
limousine

## die Tankstelle • gas station

die Zapfsäule
gas pump

der Benzinpreis
price

der Tankstellenplatz
forecourt

| **Vokabular** • vocabulary | | |
|---|---|---|
| **das Benzin**<br>gasoline | **verbleit**<br>leaded | **die Autowaschanlage**<br>car wash |
| **bleifrei**<br>unleaded | **das Öl**<br>oil | **das Frostschutzmittel**<br>antifreeze |
| **die Werkstatt**<br>garage | **der Diesel**<br>diesel | **die Scheibenwasch anlage**<br>windshield washer fluid |

**Voll tanken, bitte.**
Fill it up, please.

# das Auto 2 • car 2

## die Innenausstattung • interior

der Rücksitz
backseat

die Armstütze
armrest

die Kopfstütze
headrest

die
Türverriegelung
door lock

der Türgriff
handle

**Vokabular** • vocabulary

| | | | | |
|---|---|---|---|---|
| **zweitürig**<br>two-door | **viertürig**<br>four-door | **die Zündung**<br>ignition | **die Bremse**<br>brake | **das Gaspedal**<br>accelerator |
| **dreitürig**<br>hatchback | **mit**<br>**Handschaltung**<br>manual | **mit**<br>**Automatik**<br>automatic | **die**<br>**Kupplung**<br>clutch | **die Klimaanlage**<br>air-conditioning |

**Wie komme ich nach...?**
Can you tell me the way to...?

**Wo ist hier ein Parkplatz?**
Where is the parking lot?

**Kann ich hier parken?**
Can I park here?

# die Armaturen • controls

das
**Lenkrad**
steering
wheel

**die Hupe**
horn

**das Armaturenbrett**
dashboard

**die Warnlichter**
hazard lights

**das GPS-System**
satellite navigation

**die Linkssteuerung** | left-hand drive

die
**Temperaturanzeige**
temperature gauge

**der Drehzahlmesser**
tachometer

der
**Tachometer**
speedometer

die
**Kraftstoffanzeige**
fuel gauge

die
**Autostereoanlage**
car stereo

**der Lichtschalter**
light switch

**der Heizungsregler**
heater controls

der
**Kilometerzähler**
odometer

**der Airbag**
air bag

**der Schalthebel**
gearshift

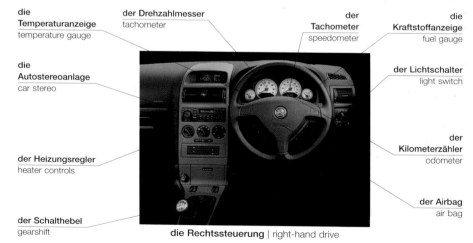

**die Rechtssteuerung** | right-hand drive

# das Auto 3 • car 3

## die Mechanik • mechanics

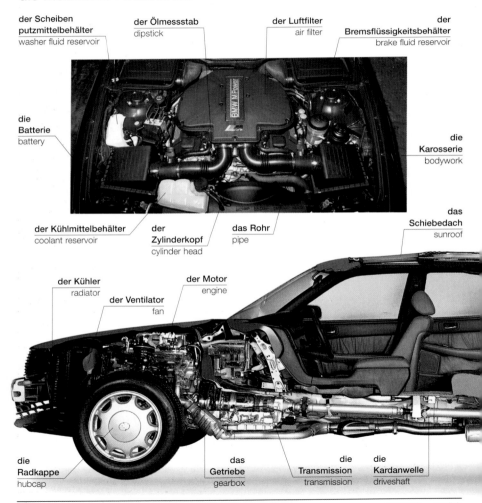

der Scheiben
putzmittelbehälter
washer fluid reservoir

der Ölmessstab
dipstick

der Luftfilter
air filter

der
Bremsflüssigkeitsbehälter
brake fluid reservoir

die
Batterie
battery

die
Karosserie
bodywork

das
Schiebedach
sunroof

der Kühlmittelbehälter
coolant reservoir

der
Zylinderkopf
cylinder head

das Rohr
pipe

der Kühler
radiator

der Motor
engine

der Ventilator
fan

die
Radkappe
hubcap

das
Getriebe
gearbox

die
Transmission
transmission

die
Kardanwelle
driveshaft

# die Reifenpanne • flat tire

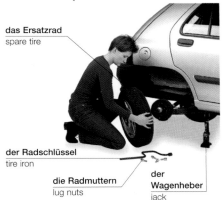

**das Ersatzrad**
spare tire

**der Radschlüssel**
tire iron

**die Radmuttern**
lug nuts

**der Wagenheber**
jack

**ein Rad wechseln**
change a tire (v)

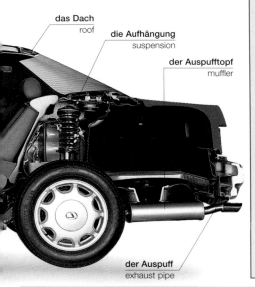

**das Dach**
roof

**die Aufhängung**
suspension

**der Auspufftopf**
muffler

**der Auspuff**
exhaust pipe

---

**Vokabular • vocabulary**

**der Autounfall**
car accident

**die Panne**
breakdown

**die Versicherung**
insurance

**der Abschleppwagen**
tow truck

**der Mechaniker**
mechanic

**der Reifendruck**
tire pressure

**der Sicherungskasten**
fuse box

**die Zündkerze**
spark plug

**der Keilriemen**
fan belt

**der Benzintank**
gas tank

**der Nockenriemen**
cam belt

**der Turbolader**
turbocharger

**der Verteiler**
distributor

**die Einstellung**
timing

**das Chassis**
chassis

**die Handbremse**
parking brake

**die Lichtmaschine**
alternator

..........................

**Ich habe eine Panne.**
My car has broken down.

**Mein Auto springt nicht an.**
My car won't start.

---

# das Motorrad • motorcycle

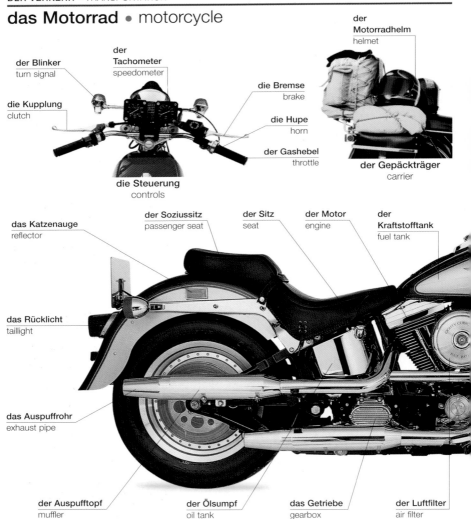

der **Blinker**
turn signal

der
**Tachometer**
speedometer

die **Kupplung**
clutch

die **Bremse**
brake

die **Hupe**
horn

der **Gashebel**
throttle

die **Steuerung**
controls

der
**Motorradhelm**
helmet

der **Gepäckträger**
carrier

das **Katzenauge**
reflector

der **Soziussitz**
passenger seat

der **Sitz**
seat

der **Motor**
engine

der
**Kraftstofftank**
fuel tank

das **Rücklicht**
taillight

das **Auspuffrohr**
exhaust pipe

der **Auspufftopf**
muffler

der **Ölsumpf**
oil tank

das **Getriebe**
gearbox

der **Luftfilter**
air filter

## die Typen • types

das Visier
visor

der Lederanzug
leathers

der
Leuchtstreifen
reflector strap

der
Knieschützer
knee pad

die Kleidung | clothing

der Scheinwerfer
headlight

die
Aufhängung
suspension

das
Schutzblech
mudguard

das Bremspedal
brake pedal

die Achse
axle

der Reifen
tire

die Rennmaschine | racing bike

die Windschutzscheibe
windshield

der Tourer | tourer

das Geländemotorrad | dirt bike

der Motor
radständer
stand

der Roller | scooter

# das Fahrrad • bicycle

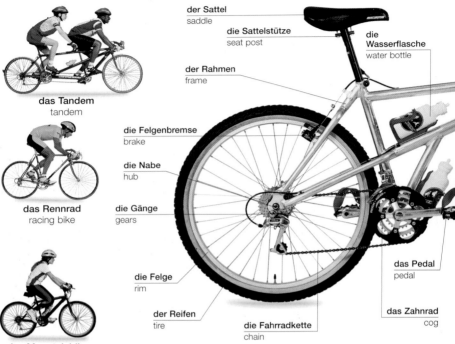

der Sattel
saddle

die Sattelstütze
seat post

die Wasserflasche
water bottle

der Rahmen
frame

die Felgenbremse
brake

die Nabe
hub

die Gänge
gears

die Felge
rim

der Reifen
tire

die Fahrradkette
chain

das Pedal
pedal

das Zahnrad
cog

das Tandem
tandem

das Rennrad
racing bike

das Mountainbike
mountain bike

das Tourenfahrrad
touring bike

der Fahrradhelm
helmet

das Straßenrad
road bike

der Fahrradweg | bike lane

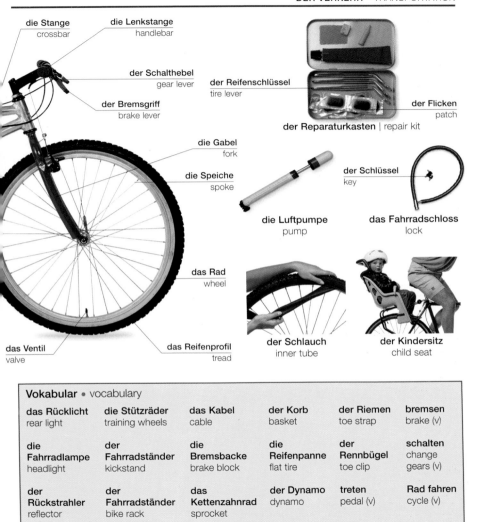

die Stange
crossbar

die Lenkstange
handlebar

der Schalthebel
gear lever

der Bremsgriff
brake lever

der Reifenschlüssel
tire lever

der Flicken
patch

**der Reparaturkasten** | repair kit

die Gabel
fork

die Speiche
spoke

der Schlüssel
key

die Luftpumpe
pump

das Fahrradschloss
lock

das Rad
wheel

der Schlauch
inner tube

der Kindersitz
child seat

das Ventil
valve

das Reifenprofil
tread

---

**Vokabular** • vocabulary

| | | | | | |
|---|---|---|---|---|---|
| **das Rücklicht**<br>rear light | **die Stützräder**<br>training wheels | **das Kabel**<br>cable | **der Korb**<br>basket | **der Riemen**<br>toe strap | **bremsen**<br>brake (v) |
| **die Fahrradlampe**<br>headlight | **der Fahrradständer**<br>kickstand | **die Bremsbacke**<br>brake block | **die Reifenpanne**<br>flat tire | **der Rennbügel**<br>toe clip | **schalten**<br>change gears (v) |
| **der Rückstrahler**<br>reflector | **der Fahrradständer**<br>bike rack | **das Kettenzahnrad**<br>sprocket | **der Dynamo**<br>dynamo | **treten**<br>pedal (v) | **Rad fahren**<br>cycle (v) |

---

# der Zug • train

der
**Wagen**
railcar

der
**Bahnsteig**
platform

der
**Kofferkuli**
cart

die
**Gleisnummer**
platform number

der **Pendler**
commuter

**der Bahnhof** | train station

## die Zugtypen • types of train

der **Führerstand**
engineer's cab

die
**Lokomotive**
engine

die **Schiene**
rail

**die Dampflokomotive**
steam train

**die Diesellokomotive** | diesel train

**die Elektrolokomotive**
electric train

**der Hochgeschwindigkeitszug**
high-speed train

**die Einschienenbahn**
monorail

**die U-Bahn**
subway

**die Straßenbahn**
tram

**der Güterzug**
freight train

die Gepäckablage
luggage rack

das Zugfenster
window

das Gleis
track

die Tür    der Sitz
door       seat

**das Abteil**
compartment

**der Lautsprecher**
public address system

der
**Fahrplan**
schedule

**die Fahrkarte**
ticket

**die Eingangssperre**
ticket gates

**der Speisewagen** | dining car

**die Bahnhofshalle** | concourse

**das Schlafabteil**
sleeping compartment

---

## Vokabular • vocabulary

**das Bahnnetz**
railroad network

**der Intercity**
express train

**die Stoßzeit**
rush hour

**der U-Bahnplan**
subway map

**die Verspätung**
delay

**der Fahrpreis**
fare

**der Fahrkartenschalter**
ticket office

**der Schaffner**
ticket inspector

**umsteigen**
transfer (v)

**die stromführende
Schiene**
live rail

**das Signal**
signal

**die Notbremse**
emergency lever

---

# das Flugzeug • aircraft

## das Verkehrsflugzeug • airliner

der Bug
nose

das Cockpit
cockpit

das Triebwerk
engine

der Rumpf
fuselage

die Tragfläche
wing

das Heck
tail

das Seitenruder
rudder

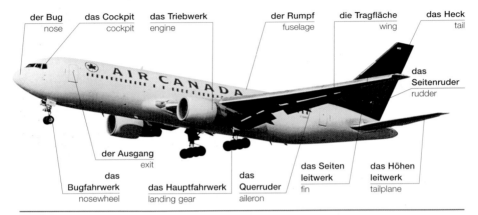

der Ausgang
exit

das Bugfahrwerk
nosewheel

das Hauptfahrwerk
landing gear

das Querruder
aileron

das Seiten leitwerk
fin

das Höhen leitwerk
tailplane

## die Kabine • cabin

der Notausgang
emergency exit

die Flugbegleiterin
flight attendant

das Gepäckfach
overhead bin

das Fenster
window

die Luftdüse
air vent

die Leselampe
reading light

der Sitz
seat

die Reihe
row

der Klapptisch
tray-table

die Armlehne
armrest

der Gang
aisle

die Rückenlehne
seat back

deutsch • english

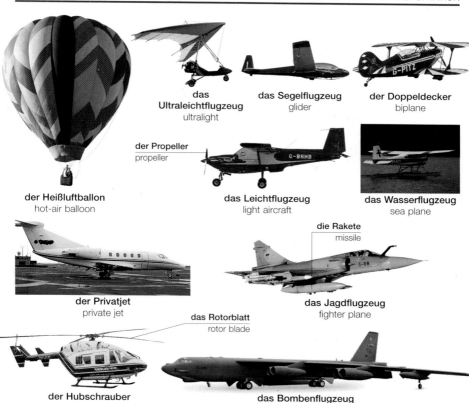

**das Ultraleichtflugzeug**
ultralight

**das Segelflugzeug**
glider

**der Doppeldecker**
biplane

**der Propeller**
propeller

**der Heißluftballon**
hot-air balloon

**das Leichtflugzeug**
light aircraft

**das Wasserflugzeug**
sea plane

**die Rakete**
missile

**der Privatjet**
private jet

**das Jagdflugzeug**
fighter plane

**das Rotorblatt**
rotor blade

**der Hubschrauber**
helicopter

**das Bombenflugzeug**
bomber

**Vokabular** • vocabulary

| | | | | |
|---|---|---|---|---|
| **der Pilot**<br>pilot | **starten**<br>take off (v) | **landen**<br>land (v) | **die Economyclass**<br>economy class | **das Handgepäck**<br>carry-on luggage |
| **der Kopilot**<br>copilot | **fliegen**<br>fly (v) | **die Höhe**<br>altitude | **die Businessclass**<br>business class | **der Sicherheitsgurt**<br>seat belt |

# der Flughafen • airport

das Vorfeld
apron

der Gepäckanhänger
baggage trailer

der Terminal
terminal

das Versorgungsfahrzeug
service vehicle

die Fluggastbrücke
jetway

**das Verkehrsflugzeug** | airliner

## Vokabular • vocabulary

| | | | |
|---|---|---|---|
| **das Gepäckband**<br>baggage carousel | **die Flugnummer**<br>flight number | **die Start- und Landebahn**<br>runway | **der Urlaub**<br>vacation |
| **der Auslandsflug**<br>international flight | **die Einwanderung**<br>immigration | **die Sicherheitsvorkehrungen**<br>security | **einen Flug buchen**<br>book a flight (v) |
| **der Inlandsflug**<br>domestic flight | **der Zoll**<br>customs | **die Gepäckröntgenmaschine**<br>X-ray machine | **einchecken**<br>check in (v) |
| **die Flugverbindung**<br>connection | **das Übergepäck**<br>excess baggage | **der Urlaubsprospekt**<br>travel brochure | **der Kontrollturm**<br>control tower |

das
**Handgepäck**
carry-on
luggage

das **Gepäck**
luggage

der **Kofferkuli**
cart

**der Abfertigungsschalter**
check-in desk

das **Visum**
visa

**der Pass** | passport

**die Passkontrolle**
passport control

die **Bordkarte**
boarding pass

das **Flugticket**
ticket

die **Gatenummer**
gate number

**die Abflughalle**
departure lounge

der **Abflug**
departures

das **Reiseziel**
destination

die **Ankunft**
arrivals

**die Fluginformationsanzeige**
information screen

**der Duty-free-Shop**
duty-free shop

**die Gepäckausgabe**
baggage claim

**der Taxistand**
taxi stand

**der Autoverleih**
car rental

# das Schiff • ship

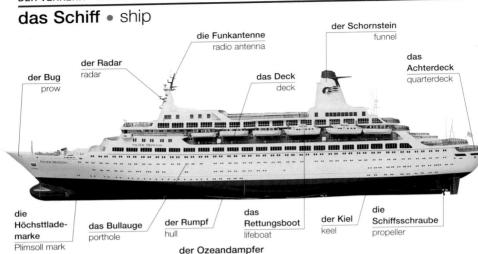

der Bug
prow

der Radar
radar

die Funkantenne
radio antenna

der Schornstein
funnel

das Deck
deck

das Achterdeck
quarterdeck

die Höchstttlade-marke
Plimsoll mark

das Bullauge
porthole

der Rumpf
hull

das Rettungsboot
lifeboat

der Kiel
keel

die Schiffsschraube
propeller

**der Ozeandampfer**
ocean liner

**die Kommandobrücke**
bridge

**der Maschinenraum**
engine room

**die Kabine**
cabin

**die Kombüse**
galley

## Vokabular • vocabulary

**das Dock**
dock

**der Hafen**
port

**die Landungsbrücke**
gangway

**der Anker**
anchor

**der Poller**
bollard

**die Ankerwinde**
windlass

**der Kapitän**
captain

**das Rennboot**
speedboat

**das Ruderboot**
rowboat

**das Kanu**
canoe

# andere Schiffe • other ships

**die Fähre**
ferry

der
**Außenbordmotor**
outboard motor

**das Schlauchboot**
inflatable dinghy

**das Tragflügelboot**
hydrofoil

**die Jacht**
yacht

**der Katamaran**
catamaran

**der Schleppdampfer**
tugboat

**das Luftkissenboot**
hovercraft

**das Containerschiff**
container ship

**die Takelung**
rigging

**das Segelboot**
sailboat

der
**Frachtraum**
hold

**das Frachtschiff**
freighter

**der Öltanker**
oil tanker

**der Flugzeugträger**
aircraft carrier

**das Kriegsschiff**
battleship

der
**Kommandoturm**
conning tower

**das U-Boot**
submarine

# der Hafen • port

das Warenlager
warehouse

der Kran
crane

der Gabelstapler
forklift

die Zufahrtßsstraße
access road

das Zollamt
customs house

das Dock
quay

der Kai
dock

die Fracht
cargo

der Container
container

der Fährterminal
ferry terminal

die Fähre
ferry

der Fahrkartenschalter
ticket office

der Passagier
passenger

**der Containerhafen** | container port

**der Passagierhafen** | passenger port

das Netz
net

das Fischerboot
fishing boat

die Verankerung
mooring

der Jachhafen
marina

**der Fischereihafen**
fishing port

**der Hafen**
harbor

**der Pier**
pier

**der Landungssteg**
jetty

**die Werft**
shipyard

die Laterne
lamp

**der Leuchtturm**
lighthouse

**die Boje**
buoy

**Vokabular** • vocabulary

| | | |
|---|---|---|
| **die Küstenwache** coast guard | **festmachen** moor (v) | **an Bord gehen** board (v) |
| **der Hafenmeister** harbor master | **anlegen** dock (v) | **von Bord gehen** disembark (v) |
| **das Trockendock** dry dock | **den Anker werfen** drop anchor (v) | **auslaufen** set sail (v) |

**der Sport**
sports

# der Football • football

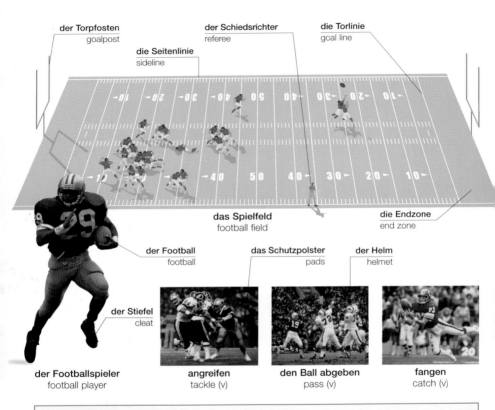

der Torpfosten
goalpost

die Seitenlinie
sideline

der Schiedsrichter
referee

die Torlinie
goal line

das Spielfeld
football field

die Endzone
end zone

der Football
football

das Schutzpolster
pads

der Helm
helmet

der Stiefel
cleat

der Footballspieler
football player

angreifen
tackle (v)

den Ball abgeben
pass (v)

fangen
catch (v)

| **Vokabular** • vocabulary | | | | |
|---|---|---|---|---|
| **die Auszeit**<br>time out | **die Mannschaft**<br>team | **die Verteidigung**<br>defense | **der Cheerleader**<br>cheerleader | **Wie ist der Stand?**<br>What is the score? |
| **das unsichere Fangen des Balls**<br>fumble | **der Angriff**<br>attack | **der Spielstand**<br>score | **der Touchdown**<br>touchdown | **Wer gewinnt?**<br>Who is winning? |

# das Rugby • rugby

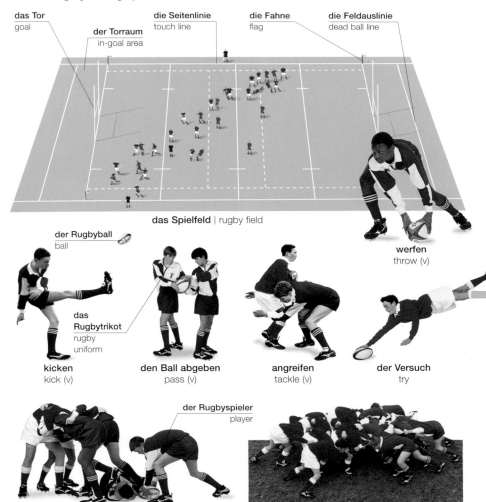

das Tor
goal

der Torraum
in-goal area

die Seitenlinie
touch line

die Fahne
flag

die Feldauslinie
dead ball line

**das Spielfeld** | rugby field

**werfen**
throw (v)

der Rugbyball
ball

das
Rugbytrikot
rugby
uniform

**kicken**
kick (v)

**den Ball abgeben**
pass (v)

**angreifen**
tackle (v)

**der Versuch**
try

der Rugbyspieler
player

**das offene Gedränge** | ruck

**das Gedränge** | scrum

# der Fußball • soccer

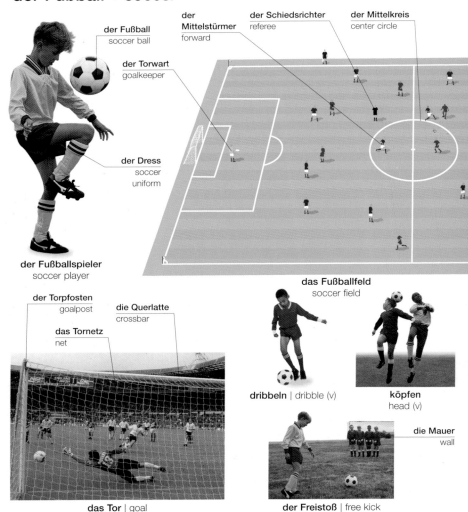

**der Fußball**
soccer ball

**der Torwart**
goalkeeper

**der Dress**
soccer uniform

**der Fußballspieler**
soccer player

**der Mittelstürmer**
forward

**der Schiedsrichter**
referee

**der Mittelkreis**
center circle

**das Fußballfeld**
soccer field

**der Torpfosten**
goalpost

**die Querlatte**
crossbar

**das Tornetz**
net

**das Tor** | goal

**dribbeln** | dribble (v)

**köpfen**
head (v)

**die Mauer**
wall

**der Freistoß** | free kick

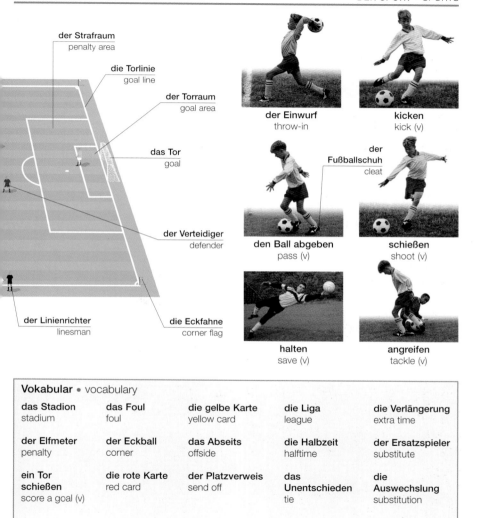

der Strafraum
penalty area

die Torlinie
goal line

der Torraum
goal area

das Tor
goal

der Verteidiger
defender

der Linienrichter
linesman

die Eckfahne
corner flag

**der Einwurf**
throw-in

**kicken**
kick (v)

der Fußballschuh
cleat

**den Ball abgeben**
pass (v)

**schießen**
shoot (v)

**halten**
save (v)

**angreifen**
tackle (v)

| **Vokabular** • vocabulary | | | | |
|---|---|---|---|---|
| **das Stadion**<br>stadium | **das Foul**<br>foul | **die gelbe Karte**<br>yellow card | **die Liga**<br>league | **die Verlängerung**<br>extra time |
| **der Elfmeter**<br>penalty | **der Eckball**<br>corner | **das Abseits**<br>offside | **die Halbzeit**<br>halftime | **der Ersatzspieler**<br>substitute |
| **ein Tor schießen**<br>score a goal (v) | **die rote Karte**<br>red card | **der Platzverweis**<br>send off | **das Unentschieden**<br>tie | **die Auswechslung**<br>substitution |

# das Hockey • hockey

## das Eishockey • ice hockey

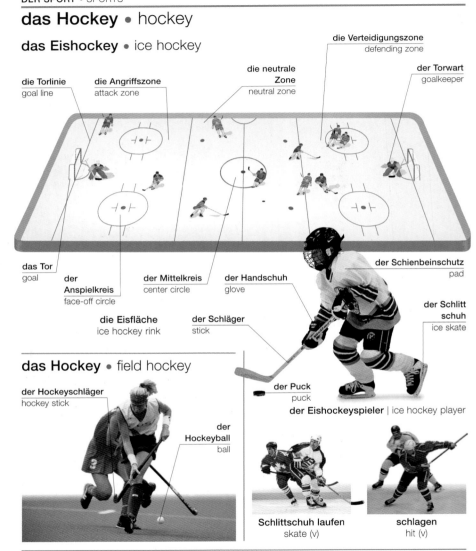

die Verteidigungszone
defending zone

der Torwart
goalkeeper

die neutrale
Zone
neutral zone

die Torlinie
goal line

die Angriffszone
attack zone

das Tor
goal

der
Anspielkreis
face-off circle

der Mittelkreis
center circle

der Handschuh
glove

die Eisfläche
ice hockey rink

der Schläger
stick

der Schienbeinschutz
pad

der Schlitt
schuh
ice skate

der Puck
puck

**der Eishockeyspieler** | ice hockey player

## das Hockey • field hockey

der Hockeyschläger
hockey stick

der
Hockeyball
ball

**Schlittschuh laufen**
skate (v)

**schlagen**
hit (v)

# das Kricket • cricket

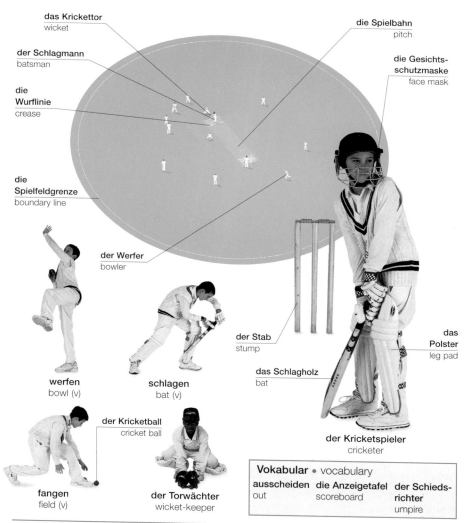

das Krickettor
wicket

die Spielbahn
pitch

der Schlagmann
batsman

die Gesichts-
schutzmaske
face mask

die
Wurflinie
crease

die
Spielfeldgrenze
boundary line

der Werfer
bowler

der Stab
stump

das
Polster
leg pad

das Schlagholz
bat

**werfen**
bowl (v)

**schlagen**
bat (v)

der Kricketspieler
cricketer

der Kricketball
cricket ball

**fangen**
field (v)

**der Torwächter**
wicket-keeper

| **Vokabular** • vocabulary | | |
|---|---|---|
| **ausscheiden** out | **die Anzeigetafel** scoreboard | **der Schieds- richter** umpire |

# der Basketball • basketball

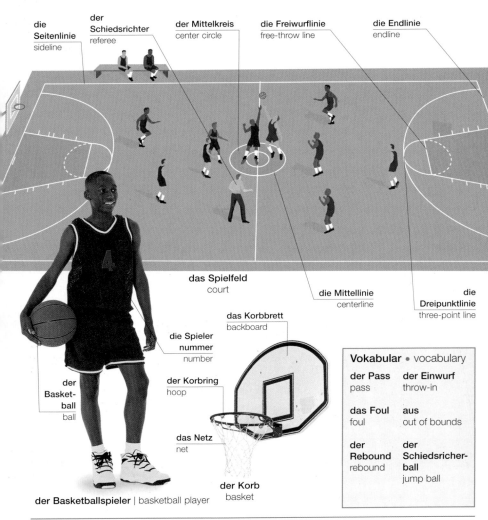

die Seitenlinie
sideline

der Schiedsrichter
referee

der Mittelkreis
center circle

die Freiwurflinie
free-throw line

die Endlinie
endline

das Spielfeld
court

die Mittellinie
centerline

die Dreipunktlinie
three-point line

die Spieler nummer
number

das Korbbrett
backboard

der Korbring
hoop

das Netz
net

der Basket-ball
ball

der Korb
basket

der Basketballspieler | basketball player

**Vokabular • vocabulary**

der Pass
pass

der Einwurf
throw-in

das Foul
foul

aus
out of bounds

der Rebound
rebound

der Schiedsricher-ball
jump ball

## die Aktionen • actions

**werfen**
throw (v)

**fangen**
catch (v)

**schießen**
shoot (v)

**springen**
jump (v)

**decken**
mark (v)

**blocken**
block (v)

**springen lassen**
dribble (v)

**einen Dunk spielen**
dunk (v)

## der Volleyball • volleyball

**blocken**
block (v)

**das Netz**
net

**baggern**
dig (v)

**der Schiedsrichter**
referee

**der Knieschützer**
knee support

**das Spielfeld** | court

# der Baseball • baseball

## das Spielfeld • field

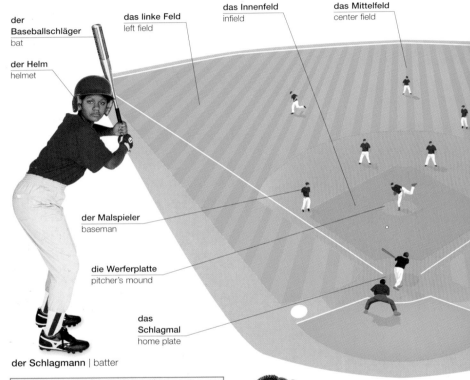

der
**Baseballschläger**
bat

**der Helm**
helmet

**das linke Feld**
left field

**das Innenfeld**
infield

**das Mittelfeld**
center field

**der Malspieler**
baseman

**die Werferplatte**
pitcher's mound

das
**Schlagmal**
home plate

**der Schlagmann** | batter

| **Vokabular** • vocabulary | | |
|---|---|---|
| **das Inning**<br>inning | **aus**<br>out | **der Schlagfehler**<br>strike |
| **der Lauf**<br>run | **in**<br>**Sicherheit**<br>safe | **der ungültige**<br>**Schlag**<br>foul ball |

**der**
**Baseball**
ball

**der Handschuh**
glove

**die Schutzmaske**
mask

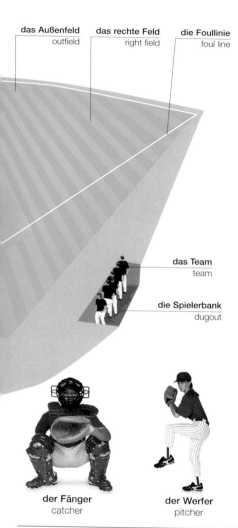

das Außenfeld
outfield

das rechte Feld
right field

die Foullinie
foul line

das Team
team

die Spielerbank
dugout

der Fänger
catcher

der Werfer
pitcher

## die Aktionen • actions

werfen | throw (v)

fangen | catch (v)

rennen
run (v)

als Fänger spielen
field (v)

rutschen
slide (v)

hinterherlaufen
tag (v)

werfen
pitch (v)

schlagen
bat (v)

der
Schieds
richter
umpire

spielen | play (v)

# das Tennis • tennis

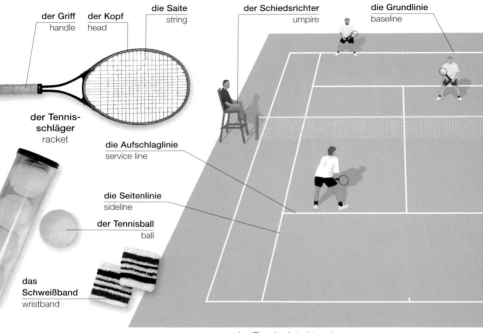

der Griff
handle

der Kopf
head

die Saite
string

der Schiedsrichter
umpire

die Grundlinie
baseline

der Tennis-
schläger
racket

die Aufschlaglinie
service line

die Seitenlinie
sideline

der Tennisball
ball

das
Schweißband
wristband

**der Tennisplatz** | tennis court

| **Vokabular** • vocabulary | | | | | |
|---|---|---|---|---|---|
| **das Einzel**<br>singles | **der Satz**<br>set | **der Einstand**<br>deuce | **der Fehler**<br>fault | **der Slice**<br>slice | **der Spin**<br>spin |
| **das Doppel**<br>doubles | **das Match**<br>match | **der Vorteil**<br>advantage | **das Ass**<br>ace | **Netz!**<br>let! | **der Linienrichter**<br>linesman |
| **das Spiel**<br>game | **der Tiebreak**<br>tiebreaker | **null**<br>love | **der Stoppball**<br>dropshot | **der Ballwechsel**<br>rally | **die Meisterschaft**<br>championship |

das Netz
net

**der Schmetterball**
smash

**der Balljunge**
ball boy

**aufschlagen**
serve (v)

die
**Tennisschuhe**
tennis shoes

**der Tennisspieler**
player

## die Schläge • strokes

**der Aufschlag**
serve

**der Volley**
volley

**der Return**
return

**der Lob**
lob

**die Vorhand**
forehand

**die Rückhand**
backhand

## die Schlägerspiele • racket games

**der Federball**
shuttlecock

**der Tischten-
nisschläger**
paddle

**das Badminton**
badminton

**das Tischtennis**
table tennis

**das Squash**
squash

**das Racquetball**
racquetball

# **das Golf** • golf

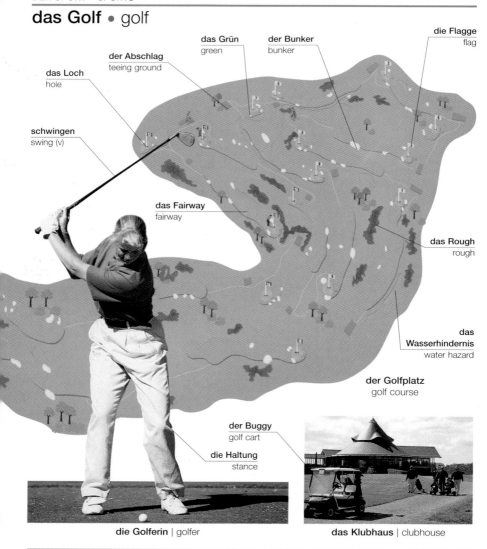

**das Grün**
green

**der Bunker**
bunker

**die Flagge**
flag

**der Abschlag**
teeing ground

**das Loch**
hole

**schwingen**
swing (v)

**das Fairway**
fairway

**das Rough**
rough

**das Wasserhindernis**
water hazard

**der Golfplatz**
golf course

**der Buggy**
golf cart

**die Haltung**
stance

**die Golferin** | golfer

**das Klubhaus** | clubhouse

# die Ausrüstung • equipment

## die Golf- schläger • golf clubs

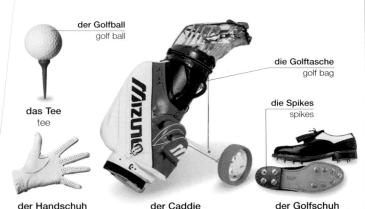

**der Golfball**
golf ball

**das Tee**
tee

**die Golftasche**
golf bag

**die Spikes**
spikes

**der Handschuh**
glove

**der Caddie**
bag cart

**der Golfschuh**
golf shoe

**das Holz**
wood

**der Putter**
putter

**das Eisen**
iron

# die Aktionen • actions

**vom Abschlag spielen**
tee off (v)

**driven**
drive (v)

**einlochen**
putt (v)

**chippen**
chip (v)

**das Wedge**
wedge

---

**Vokabular** • vocabulary

| | | | | | |
|---|---|---|---|---|---|
| **das Par**<br>par | **über Par**<br>over par | **das Golfturnier**<br>tournament | **der Caddie**<br>caddy | **der Schlag**<br>stroke | **die Spielbahn**<br>line of play |
| **unter Par**<br>under par | **das Hole-in-One**<br>hole in one | **das Handicap**<br>handicap | **die Zuschauer**<br>spectators | **der Übungsschwung**<br>practice swing | **der Durchschwung**<br>backswing |

---

# die Leichtathletik • track and field

**die Bahn**
lane

**die Rennbahn**
track

**die Ziellinie**
finish line

**die Startlinie**
starting line

**der Sportplatz**
field

**der Startblock**
starting blocks

**der Sprinter**
sprinter

**die Leichtathletin**
athlete

**das Diskuswerfen**
discus

**das Kugelstoßen**
shotput

**das Speerwerfen**
javelin

| **Vokabular** • vocabulary | | | |
|---|---|---|---|
| **das Rennen**<br>race | **der Rekord**<br>record | **das Fotofinish**<br>photo finish | **der Stabhochsprung**<br>pole vault |
| **die Zeit**<br>time | **einen Rekord brechen**<br>break a record (v) | **der Marathon**<br>marathon | **die persönliche Bestleistung**<br>personal best |

**die Stoppuhr**
stopwatch

**der Stab**
baton

**die Latte**
crossbar

**der Staffellauf**
relay race

**der Hochsprung**
high jump

**der Weitsprung**
long jump

**der Hürdenlauf**
hurdles

## das Turnen • gymnastics

**das Sprungbrett**
springboard

**die Turnerin**
gymnast

**das Pferd**
horse

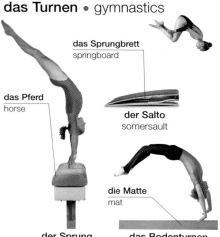

**der Salto**
somersault

**der Schwebebalken**
beam

**das Gymnastikband**
ribbon

**die Matte**
mat

**der Sprung**
vault

**das Bodenturnen**
floor exercises

**das Rad**
cartwheel

**die rhythmische Gymnastik**
rhythmic gymnastics

---

### Vokabular • vocabulary

| | | | | |
|---|---|---|---|---|
| **das Reck**<br>horizontal bar | **der Stufenbarren**<br>asymmetric bars | **die Ringe**<br>rings | **die Medaillen**<br>medals | **das Silber**<br>silver |
| **der Barren**<br>parallel bars | **das Seitpferd**<br>pommel horse | **das Siegerpodium**<br>podium | **das Gold**<br>gold | **die Bronze**<br>bronze |

---

# der Kampfsport • combat sports

der Gegner
opponent

der Kopfschutz
guard

**das Karate**
karate

der Handschuh
glove

der Gürtel
belt

**das Taekwondo**
tae kwon do

**das Judo**
judo

die Maske
mask

der Säbel
sword

**das Aikido**
aikido

**das Kendo**
kendo

**das Kung-Fu**
kung fu

**das Kickboxen**
kickboxing

**das Ringen**
wrestling

**das Boxen**
boxing

# die Techniken • actions

**das Fallen**
fall

**der Griff**
hold

**der Wurf**
throw

**das Fesseln**
pin

**der Seitfußstoß**
kick

**der Stoß**
punch

**der Angriff**
strike

**der Sprung**
jump

**der Block**
block

**der Hieb**
chop

---

### Vokabular • vocabulary

| | | | | |
|---|---|---|---|---|
| **der Boxring**<br>boxing ring | **die Runde**<br>round | **die Faust**<br>fist | **der schwarze Gürtel**<br>black belt | **die Capoeira**<br>capoeira |
| **die Boxhandschuhe**<br>boxing gloves | **der Kampf**<br>bout | **der Knockout**<br>knockout | **die Selbstverteidigung**<br>self-defense | **das Sumo**<br>sumo wrestling |
| **der Mundschutz**<br>mouth guard | **das Sparring**<br>sparring | **der Sandsack**<br>punching bag | **die Kampfsportarten**<br>martial arts | **das Thai-Chi**<br>tai chi |

# der Schwimmsport • swimming
## die Ausrüstung • equipment

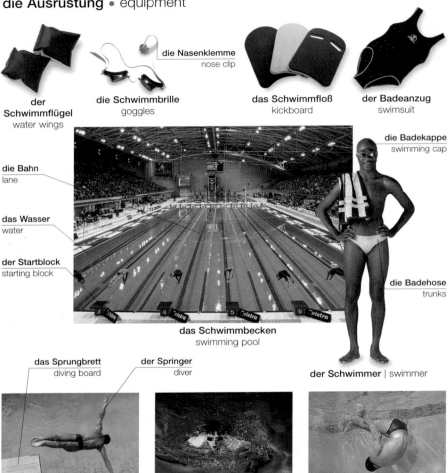

**der Schwimmflügel**
water wings

**die Schwimmbrille**
goggles

**die Nasenklemme**
nose clip

**das Schwimmfloß**
kickboard

**der Badeanzug**
swimsuit

**die Badekappe**
swimming cap

**die Bahn**
lane

**das Wasser**
water

**der Startblock**
starting block

**die Badehose**
trunks

**das Schwimmbecken**
swimming pool

**das Sprungbrett**
diving board

**der Springer**
diver

**der Schwimmer** | swimmer

**springen** | dive (v)

**schwimmen** | swim (v)

**die Wende** | turn

# die Schwimmstile • styles

**das Kraulen**
front crawl

**das Brustschwimmen**
breaststroke

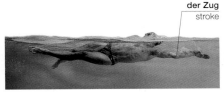

der Zug
stroke

**das Rückenschwimmen** | backstroke

der Stoß
kick

**der Butterfly** | butterfly

# das Tauchen • scuba diving

die Druckluftflasche
air cylinder

der Taucheranzug
wetsuit

die
Tauchermaske
mask

die
Schwimmflosse
fin

der
Lungenautomat
regulator

der Bleigürtel
weight belt

der Schnorchel
snorkel

## Vokabular • vocabulary

| | | | | | |
|---|---|---|---|---|---|
| **der Sprung** dive | **Wasser treten** tread water (v) | **das tiefe Ende** deep end | **der Wasserball** water polo | **das flache Ende** shallow end | **der Krampf** cramp |
| **der Turmsprung** high dive | **der Startsprung** racing dive | **die Schließfächer** lockers | **der Bademeister** lifeguard | **das Synchronschwimmen** synchronized swimming | **ertrinken** drown (v) |

# der Segelsport • sailing

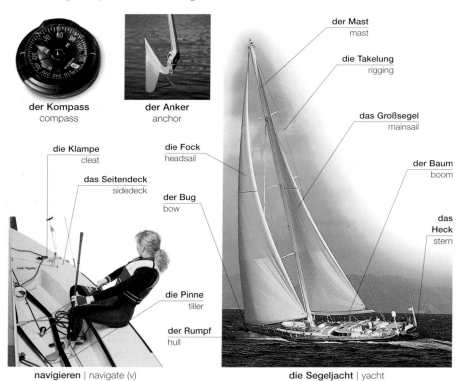

**der Kompass**
compass

**der Anker**
anchor

**der Mast**
mast

**die Takelung**
rigging

**das Großsegel**
mainsail

**die Fock**
headsail

**die Klampe**
cleat

**das Seitendeck**
sidedeck

**der Bug**
bow

**der Baum**
boom

**das Heck**
stern

**die Pinne**
tiller

**der Rumpf**
hull

**navigieren** | navigate (v)

**die Segeljacht** | yacht

## die Sicherheit • safety

**die Leuchtrakete**
flare

**der Rettungsring**
life buoy

**die Schwimmweste**
life jacket

**das Rettungsboot**
life raft

# der Wassersport • watersports

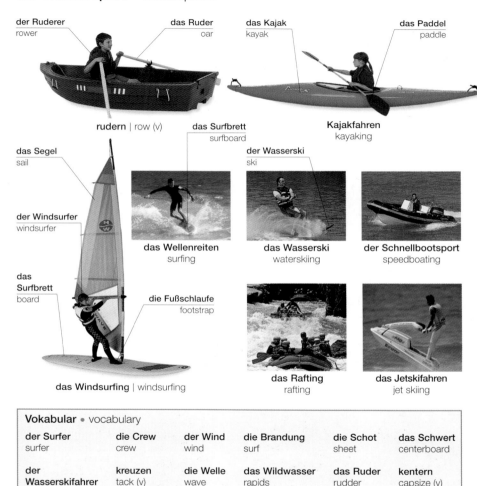

der Ruderer
rower

das Ruder
oar

das Kajak
kayak

das Paddel
paddle

**rudern** | row (v)

**Kajakfahren**
kayaking

das Surfbrett
surfboard

das Segel
sail

der Wasserski
ski

der Windsurfer
windsurfer

das
Surfbrett
board

die Fußschlaufe
footstrap

**das Wellenreiten**
surfing

**das Wasserski**
waterskiing

**der Schnellbootsport**
speedboating

**das Windsurfing** | windsurfing

**das Rafting**
rafting

**das Jetskifahren**
jet skiing

**Vokabular** • vocabulary

| | | | | | |
|---|---|---|---|---|---|
| **der Surfer**<br>surfer | **die Crew**<br>crew | **der Wind**<br>wind | **die Brandung**<br>surf | **die Schot**<br>sheet | **das Schwert**<br>centerboard |
| **der Wasserskifahrer**<br>waterskier | **kreuzen**<br>tack (v) | **die Welle**<br>wave | **das Wildwasser**<br>rapids | **das Ruder**<br>rudder | **kentern**<br>capsize (v) |

# der Reitsport • horseback riding

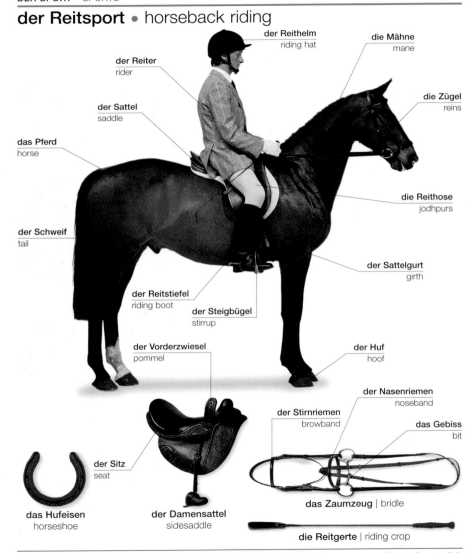

der Reithelm
riding hat

die Mähne
mane

der Reiter
rider

die Zügel
reins

der Sattel
saddle

das Pferd
horse

die Reithose
jodhpurs

der Schweif
tail

der Sattelgurt
girth

der Reitstiefel
riding boot

der Steigbügel
stirrup

der Vorderzwiesel
pommel

der Huf
hoof

der Nasenriemen
noseband

der Stirnriemen
browband

das Gebiss
bit

der Sitz
seat

das Hufeisen
horseshoe

der Damensattel
sidesaddle

das Zaumzeug | bridle

die Reitgerte | riding crop

# die Veranstaltungen • events

das Rennpferd
racehorse

das Hindernis
fence

**das Pferderennen**
horse race

**das Jagdrennen**
steeplechase

**das Trabrennen**
harness race

**das Rodeo**
rodeo

**das Springreiten**
showjumping

**das Zweispännerrennen**
carriage race

**das Wanderreiten**
trail riding

**das Dressurreiten**
dressage

**das Polo**
polo

## Vokabular • vocabulary

| | | | | | |
|---|---|---|---|---|---|
| **der Schritt**<br>walk | **der Kanter**<br>canter | **der Sprung**<br>jump | **das Halfter**<br>halter | **die Koppel**<br>paddock | **das Flachrennen**<br>flat race |
| **der Trab**<br>trot | **der Galopp**<br>gallop | **der Stallbursche**<br>groom | **der Pferdestall**<br>stable | **der Turnierplatz**<br>arena | **die Rennbahn**<br>racecourse |

# der Angelsport • fishing

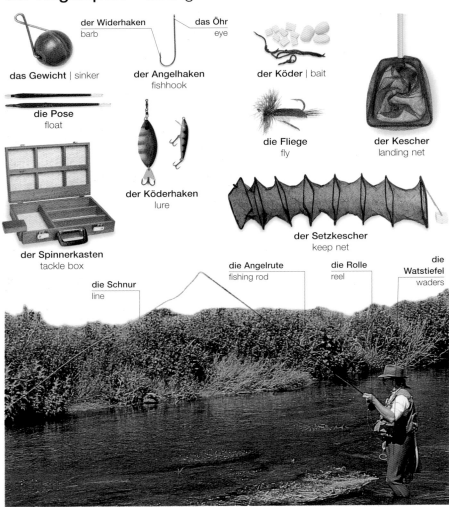

**der Widerhaken**
barb

**das Öhr**
eye

**das Gewicht** | sinker

**der Angelhaken**
fishhook

**der Köder** | bait

**die Pose**
float

**die Fliege**
fly

**der Kescher**
landing net

**der Köderhaken**
lure

**der Setzkescher**
keep net

**der Spinnerkasten**
tackle box

**die Angelrute**
fishing rod

**die Rolle**
reel

**die
Watstiefel**
waders

**die Schnur**
line

**der Angler** | angler

# die Fischfangarten • types of fishing

**das Süßwasserangeln**
freshwater fishing

**das Fliegenangeln**
fly fishing

**das Sportangeln**
sport fishing

**die Hochseefischerei**
deep sea fishing

**das Brandungsangeln**
surfcasting

# die Aktivitäten • activities

**auswerfen**
cast (v)

**fangen**
catch (v)

**einholen**
reel in (v)

**mit dem Netz fangen**
net (v)

**loslassen**
release (v)

---

**Vokabular** • vocabulary

| | | | | |
|---|---|---|---|---|
| **ködern**<br>bait (v) | **die Angelgeräte**<br>tackle | **die Regenhaut**<br>rain gear | **der Angelschein**<br>fishing license | **der Fischkorb**<br>creel |
| **anbeißen**<br>bite (v) | **die Rolle**<br>spool | **die Stake**<br>pole | **die Seefischerei**<br>marine fishing | **das Speerfischen**<br>spearfishing |

---

# der Skisport • skiing

**der Skihang**
ski slope

**der Sessellift**
chairlift

**der Kabinenlift**
cable car

**der Handschuh**
glove

**die Skipiste**
ski run

**die Sicherheitssperre**
safety barrier

**der Skistock**
ski pole

**die Spitze**
tip

**die Kante**
edge

**der Ski**
ski

**die Skijacke**
ski jacket

**die Skiläuferin**
skier

**der Skistiefel**
ski boot

# die Disziplinen • events

**der Abfahrtslauf**
downhill skiing

**das Tor**
gate

**der Slalom**
slalom

**der Skisprung**
ski jump

**der Langlauf**
cross-country skiing

# der Wintersport • winter sports

**das Eisklettern**
ice climbing

**das Eislaufen**
ice-skating

**die Skibrille**
goggles

**der Schlittschuh**
skate

**der Eiskunstlauf**
figure skating

**das Snowboarding**
snowboarding

**der Bobsport**
bobsled

**das Rennrodeln**
luge

**das Schneemobil**
snowmobile

**das Schlittenfahren**
sledding

**Vokabular** • vocabulary

| | |
|---|---|
| **die alpine Kombination** <br> alpine skiing | **das Hundeschlittenfahren** <br> dogsledding |
| **der Riesenslalom** <br> giant slalom | **das Eisschnelllauf** <br> speed skating |
| **abseits der Piste** <br> off-piste | **das Biathlon** <br> biathlon |
| **das Curling** <br> curling | **die Lawine** <br> avalanche |

# die anderen Sportarten • other sports

das Segelflugzeug
glider

der Drachen
hang-glider

**das Segelfliegen**
gliding

der Fallschirm
parachute

**das Drachenfliegen**
hang-gliding

das Seil
rope

**das Klettern**
rock climbing

**das Fallschirmspringen**
parachuting

**das Gleitschirmfliegen**
paragliding

**das Fallschirmspringen**
skydiving

**das Abseilen**
rappelling

**das Bungeejumping**
bungee jumping

der
**Rennfahrer**
race-car driver

**das Rallyefahren**
rally driving

**der Rennsport**
auto racing

**das Motocross**
motocross

**das Motorradrennen**
motorcycle racing

**das Skateboard**
skateboard

der **Lacrosseschläger**
stick

**das Florett**
foil

**die Maske**
mask

**das Skateboard-
fahren**
skateboarding

**das Inlineskaten**
inline skating

**das Lacrosse**
lacrosse

**das Fechten**
fencing

**der Kegel**
pin

die **Zielscheibe**
target

**der Bogen**
bow

**der Pfeil**
arrow

**der Köcher**
quiver

**das Bogenschießen**
archery

**das
Scheibenschießen**
target shooting

die
**Bowlingkugel**
bowling ball

**das Bowling**
bowling

**das Poolbillard**
pool

**das Snooker**
snooker

# die Fitness • fitness

**das Trainingsrad**
exercise bike

**das Fitnessgerät**
gym machine

**die Bank**
bench

**die Gewichte**
free weights

**die Stange**
bar

**das Fitnesscenter** | gym

**die Rudermaschine**
rowing machine

**das Laufband**
treadmill

**die Langlaufmaschine**
elliptical trainer

**die private Fitness-trainerin**
personal trainer

**die Tretmaschine**
stair machine

**das Schwimmbecken**
swimming pool

**die Sauna**
sauna

# die Übungen • exercises

**das Strecken**
stretch

**der Ausfall**
lunge

**die Strumpfhose**
tights

**der Liegestütz**
push-up

**die Kniebeuge**
squat

**das Rumpfheben**
sit-up

**die Hantel**
dumbbell

**die Bizepsübung**
bicep curl

**der Beinstütz**
leg press

**die Brustübung**
chest press

**Trainings schuhe**
sneakers

**die Gewicht hantel**
weight bar

**das Krafttraining**
weight training

**das Jogging**
jogging

**das Pilates**
Pilates

---

**Vokabular** • vocabulary

| | | | | |
|---|---|---|---|---|
| **trainieren**<br>train (v) | **beugen**<br>flex (v) | **ausstrecken**<br>extend (v) | **die Boxgymnastik**<br>boxercise | **das Seilspringen**<br>jumping rope |
| **sich aufwärmen**<br>warm up (v) | **auf der Stelle joggen**<br>jog in place (v) | **hochziehen**<br>pull up (v) | **das Zirkeltraining**<br>circuit training | |

---

**die Freizeit**
leisure

# das Theater • theater

der Vorhang
curtain

die Kulisse
wings

das Bühnenbild
set

das Publikum
audience

das Orchester
orchestra

**die Bühne** | stage

der Sitzplatz
seat

der zweite Rang
balcony seats

die Reihe
row

die Loge
box

der erste Rang
mezzanine

der Balkon
balcony

der Gang
aisle

das Parkett
orchestra seats

**die Bestuhlung** | seating

## Vokabular • vocabulary

| | | |
|---|---|---|
| **das Theaterstück** play | **der Produzent** director | **die Premiere** opening night |
| **die Besetzung** cast | **der Prospekt** backdrop | **die Pause** intermission |
| **der Schauspieler** actor | **das Rollenheft** script | **das Programm** program |
| **die Schauspielerin** actress | **der Regisseur** producer | **der Orchestergraben** orchestra pit |

**das Konzert**
concert

**das Musical**
musical

das
**Theaterkostüm**
costume

**das Ballett**
ballet

**Vokabular** • vocabulary

**der Platzanweiser**
usher

**die klassische Musik**
classical music

**die Noten**
musical score

**der Soundtrack**
soundtrack

**applaudieren**
applaud (v)

**die Zugabe**
encore

**Ich möchte zwei Karten für die Aufführung heute Abend.**
I'd like two tickets for tonight's performance.

**Um wie viel Uhr beginnt die Aufführung?**
What time does it start?

**die Oper**
opera

## das Kino • movies

das
**Popcorn**
popcorn

**die Kasse**
box office

**das Plakat**
poster

**das Foyer**
lobby

**der Kinosaal**
movie theater

**die Leinwand**
screen

**Vokabular** • vocabulary

**die Komödie**
comedy

**der Thriller**
thriller

**der Horrorfilm**
horror movie

**der Western**
Western

**der Liebesfilm**
romance

**der Science-Fiction-Film**
science fiction movie

**der Abenteuerfilm**
adventure movie

**der Zeichentrickfilm**
animated movie

# das Orchester • orchestra

## die Saiteninstrumente • strings

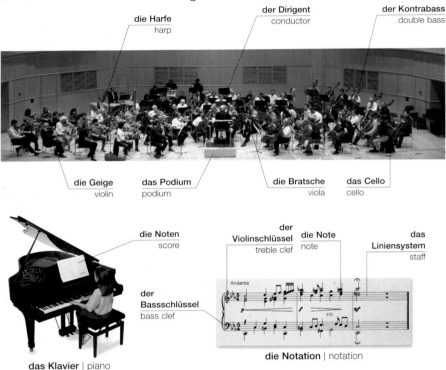

die Harfe
harp

der Dirigent
conductor

der Kontrabass
double bass

die Geige
violin

das Podium
podium

die Bratsche
viola

das Cello
cello

die Noten
score

der Violinschlüssel
treble clef

die Note
note

das Liniensystem
staff

der Bassschlüssel
bass clef

die **Notation** | notation

das **Klavier** | piano

---

**Vokabular** • vocabulary

| | | | | | |
|---|---|---|---|---|---|
| **die Ouvertüre**<br>overture | **die Sonate**<br>sonata | **die Tonhöhe**<br>pitch | **das Kreuz**<br>sharp | **der Taktstrich**<br>bar | **die Tonleiter**<br>scale |
| **die Symphonie**<br>symphony | **die Musikinstrumente**<br>instruments | **das Pausenzeichen**<br>rest | **das B**<br>flat | **das Auflösungszeichen**<br>natural | **der Taktstock**<br>baton |

---

## die Holzblasinstrumente • woodwind

**die Pikkoloflöte**
piccolo

**die Querflöte**
flute

**die Oboe**
oboe

**das Englischhorn**
English horn

**die Klarinette**
clarinet

**die Bassklarinette**
bass clarinet

**das Fagott**
bassoon

**das Kontrafagott**
double bassoon

**das Saxofon**
saxophone

## die Schlaginstrumente • percussion

**das Vibrafon**
vibraphone

**die Bongos**
bongos

**die kleine Trommel**
snare drum

**die Kesselpauke**
kettledrum

**der Gong**
gong

**das Becken**
cymbals

**das Tamburin**
tambourine

**der Triangel**
triangle

**die Maracas**
maracas

**das Fußpedal**
foot pedal

## die Blechblasinstrumente • brass

**die Trompete**
trumpet

**die Posaune**
trombone

**das Horn**
French horn

**die Tuba**
tuba

# das Konzert • concert

der Lautsprecher
speaker

die Fans
fans

der
Leadsänger
lead singer

der Gitarrist
guitarist

das
Mikrophon
microphone

der
Schlag-zeuger
drummer

**das Rockkonzert** | rock concert

# die Instrumente • instruments

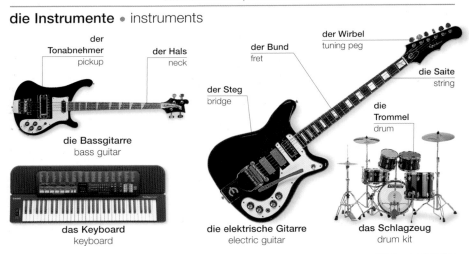

der
Tonabnehmer
pickup

der Hals
neck

der Bund
fret

der Wirbel
tuning peg

die Saite
string

der Steg
bridge

die
Trommel
drum

**die Bassgitarre**
bass guitar

**das Keyboard**
keyboard

**die elektrische Gitarre**
electric guitar

**das Schlagzeug**
drum kit

# die Musikstile • musical styles

**der Jazz**
jazz

**der Blues**
blues

**die Punkmusik**
punk

**der Folk**
folk music

**der Pop**
pop

**die Tanzmusik**
dance

**der Rap**
rap

**das Heavy Metal**
heavy metal

**die klassische Musik**
classical music

| **Vokabular** • vocabulary | | | | | | |
|---|---|---|---|---|---|---|
| **das Lied** | **der Text** | **die Melodie** | **der Beat** | **der Reggae** | **die Countrymusic** | **Scheinwerfer** |
| song | lyrics | melody | beat | reggae | country | spotlight |

# die Besichtigungstour • sightseeing

der Tourist
tourist

die Route
itinerary

mit offenem
Oberdeck
open-top

der Stadtrundfahrtbus | tour bus

der
Fremdenführer
tour guide

die Figur
figurine

die Führung
guided tour

die Andenken
souvenirs

die Touristenattraktion | tourist attraction

---

## Vokabular • vocabulary

| | | | | |
|---|---|---|---|---|
| **geöffnet**<br>open | **der Film**<br>film | **der Camcorder**<br>camcorder | **links**<br>left | **Wo ist…?**<br>Where is…? |
| **geschlossen**<br>closed | **die Batterien**<br>batteries | **die Kamera**<br>camera | **rechts**<br>right | **Ich habe mich verlaufen.**<br>I'm lost. |
| **das Eintrittsgeld**<br>entrance fee | **der Reiseführer**<br>guidebook | **die Richtungs-angaben**<br>directions | **geradeaus**<br>straight ahead | **Können Sie mir sagen, wie ich nach…komme?**<br>Can you tell me the way to…? |

---

# die Sehenswürdigkeiten • attractions

**das Gemälde**
painting

**das Aussellungs stück**
exhibit

**die Ausstellung**
exhibition

**die berühmte Ruine**
famous ruin

**die Kunstgalerie**
art gallery

**das Monument**
monument

**das Museum**
museum

**das historische Gebäude**
historic building

**das Kasino**
casino

**der Park**
gardens

**der Nationalpark**
national park

# die Information • information

**die Zeiten**
times

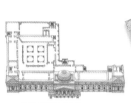

**der Grundriss**
floor plan

**der Stadtplan**
map

**der Fahrplan**
schedule

**die Touristeninformation**
tourist information

# die Aktivitäten im Freien • outdoor activities

**der Fußweg**
footpath

**die Sonnenuhr**
sundial

**das Café**
café

**der Park** | park

**das Gras**
grass

**die Bank**
bench

**die Gartenanlagen**
formal gardens

**die Berg-und-Talbahn**
roller coaster

**der Jahrmarkt**
fairground

**der Vergnügungspark**
theme park

**der Safaripark**
safari park

**der Zoo**
zoo

## die Aktivitäten • activites

**das Radfahren**
cycling

**das Jogging**
jogging

**das Skateboardfahren**
skateboarding

**das Inlinerfahren**
rollerblading

**der Reitweg**
bridle path

**das Vogelbeobachten**
bird-watching

**das Reiten**
horseback riding

**das Wandern**
hiking

**der Pick-nickkorb**
hamper

**das Picknick**
picnic

## der Spielplatz • playground

**der Sandkasten**
sandbox

**das Planschbecken**
wading pool

**die Schaukel**
swing

**die Wippe** | seesaw

**die Rutsche**
slide

**das Klettergerüst**
climbing frame

# der Strand • beach

das
**Hotel**
hotel

der
**Sonnenschirm**
beach umbrella

das
**Strandhäuschen**
beach hut

**der Sand**
sand

**die Welle**
wave

**das Meer**
sea

**die Strandtasche**
beach bag

**der Bikini**
bikini

**sonnenbaden** | sunbathe (v)

der
**Rettungsschwimmer**
lifeguard

**der Rettungsturm**
lifeguard tower

**der Windschutz**
windbreak

**die Promenade**
boardwalk

**der Liegestuhl**
deck chair

**die Sonnenbrille**
sunglasses

**der Sonnenhut**
sun hat

**die Sonnencreme**
suntan lotion

**der Sonnenblocker**
sunblock

**der Wasserball**
beach ball

**der Schwimmreifen**
inflatable ring

**der Badeanzug**
swimsuit

**die Schaufel**
shovel

**der Eimer**
pail

**die Sandburg**
sandcastle

**die Muschel**
shell

**das Strandtuch**
beach towel

# das Camping • camping

**die Toiletten**
restrooms

**die Mülleimer**
waste disposal

**die Duschen**
shower block

**der Stromanschluss**
electric hookup

**das Überdach**
flysheet

**der Hering**
tent peg

**der Campingplatz**
campground

**die Zeltspannleine**
guy rope

**der Wohnwagen**
camper

## Vokabular • vocabulary

**zelten**
camp (v)

**Zeltplätze frei**
sites available

**voll**
full

**die Campingplatzverwaltung**
site manager's office

**der Zeltplatz**
site

**die Zeltstange**
tent pole

**das Faltbett**
camp bed

**ein Zelt aufschlagen**
pitch a tent (v)

**die Picknickbank**
picnic bench

**die Hängematte**
hammock

**das Wohnmobil**
camper van

**der Anhänger**
trailer

**die Holzkohle**
charcoal

**der Feueranzünder**
firelighter

**ein Feuer machen**
light a fire (v)

**das Lagerfeuer**
campfire

**das Gestänge**
frame

**der Zeltboden**
ground sheet

**der Rucksack**
backpack

**die Thermos flasche**
vacuum flask

**die Wasserflasche**
water bottle

**das Zelt**
tent

**der Insektenspray**
insect repellent

**die Taschenlampe**
flashlight

**das Moskitonetz**
mosquito net

**die Thermowäsche**
thermal underwear

**die Wanderschuhe**
hiking boots

**die Regenhaut**
rain gear

**der Schlafsack**
sleeping bag

**der Gasbrenner**
camping stove

**der Grill**
barbecue grill

**die Schlafmatte**
sleeping mat

**die Luftmatratze** | air mattress

# die Privatunterhaltung • home entertainment

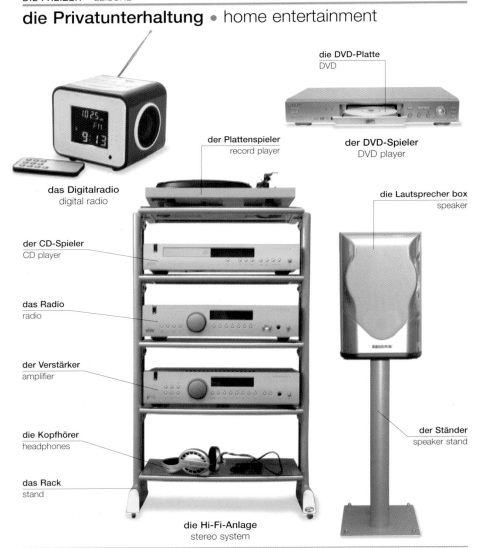

**die DVD-Platte**
DVD

**der DVD-Spieler**
DVD player

**der Plattenspieler**
record player

**das Digitalradio**
digital radio

**die Lautsprecher box**
speaker

**der CD-Spieler**
CD player

**das Radio**
radio

**der Verstärker**
amplifier

**die Kopfhörer**
headphones

**das Rack**
stand

**der Ständer**
speaker stand

**die Hi-Fi-Anlage**
stereo system

der **Bildschirm**
screen

das **Okular**
eyecup

die **Digitale Box**
DTV converter box

der **Camcorder**
camcorder

die **Satellitenschüssel**
satellite dish

der **Flachbildfernseher**
flatscreen TV

die **Spielkonsole**
console

der **Vorlauf**
fast-forward

die **Pause**
pause

die **Aufnahme**
record

die **Lautstärke**
volume

der **Rücklauf**
rewind

der **Stop**
stop

das **Abspielen**
play

der **Controller**
controller

das **Videospiel** | video game

die **Fernbedienung**
remote control

---

**Vokabular** • vocabulary

| die **CD-Platte**<br>CD | die **Werbung**<br>advertisement | das **Kabelfernsehen**<br>cable television | **digital**<br>digital | **stereo**<br>stereo |
|---|---|---|---|---|
| die **Kassette**<br>cassette tape | der **Pay-Kanal**<br>pay-per-view channel | das **Programm**<br>program | **fernsehen**<br>watch television (v) | das **Radio einstellen**<br>tune the radio (v) |
| der **Kassettenrekorder**<br>cassette player | das **Streaming**<br>streaming | den **Kanal wechseln**<br>change channel (v) | den **Fernseher einschalten**<br>turn on the television (v) | den **Fernseher abschalten**<br>turn off the television (v) |
| der **Spielfilm**<br>feature film | **WLAN**<br>Wi-Fi | **hochauflösend**<br>high-definition | | |

# die Fotografie • photography

der Auslöser
shutter release

der Blendenregler
aperture dial

die Linse
lens

der Filter
filter

die Schutzkappe
lens cap

**die Spiegelreflexkamera** | SLR camera

der Elektronenblitz
flash gun

der Belichtungsmesser
light meter

das Wechselobjektiv
zoom lens

das Stativ
tripod

# die Fotoapparattypen • types of camera

die Polaroidkamera
Polaroid camera

die Digitalkamera
digital camera

der Blitz
flash

das Kamera-Handy
camera phone

die Einwegkamera
disposable camera

# fotografieren • photograph (v)

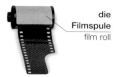

**die Filmspule**
film roll

**der Film**
film

**einstellen**
focus (v)

**entwickeln**
develop (v)

**das Negativ**
negative

**quer**
landscape

**hoch**
portrait

**das Foto** | photograph

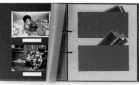

**das Fotoalbum**
photo album

**der Fotorahmen**
picture frame

# die Probleme • problems

**unterbelichtet**
underexposed

**überbelichtet**
overexposed

**unscharf**
out of focus

**die Rotfärbung der Augen**
red eye

---

**Vokabular** • vocabulary

| | |
|---|---|
| **der Bildsucher** viewfinder | **der Abzug** print |
| **die Kameratasche** camera case | **matt** matte |
| **die Belichtung** exposure | **hochglanz** gloss |
| **die Dunkelkammer** darkroom | **die Vergrößerung** enlargement |

**Könnten Sie diesen Film entwickeln lassen?**
I'd like this film processed.

---

# die Spiele • games

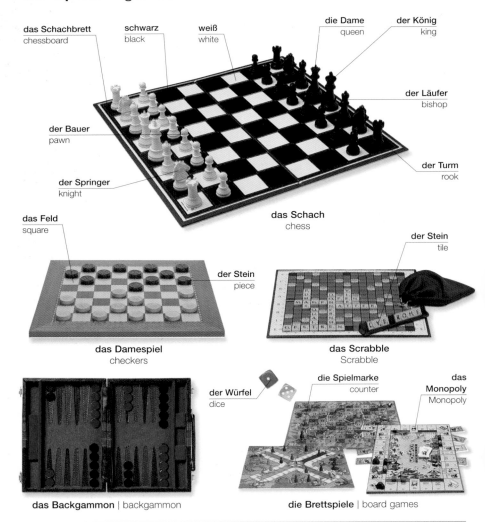

das Schachbrett
chessboard

schwarz
black

weiß
white

die Dame
queen

der König
king

der Läufer
bishop

der Bauer
pawn

der Springer
knight

der Turm
rook

das Feld
square

das Schach
chess

der Stein
piece

das Damespiel
checkers

der Stein
tile

das Scrabble
Scrabble

der Würfel
dice

die Spielmarke
counter

das Monopoly
Monopoly

das Backgammon | backgammon

die Brettspiele | board games

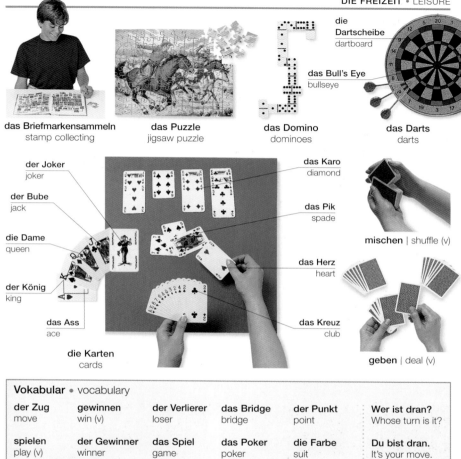

**das Briefmarkensammeln**
stamp collecting

**das Puzzle**
jigsaw puzzle

**das Domino**
dominoes

**das Darts**
darts

**die Dartscheibe**
dartboard

**das Bull's Eye**
bullseye

**der Joker**
joker

**der Bube**
jack

**die Dame**
queen

**der König**
king

**das Ass**
ace

**die Karten**
cards

**das Karo**
diamond

**das Pik**
spade

**das Herz**
heart

**das Kreuz**
club

**mischen** | shuffle (v)

**geben** | deal (v)

**Vokabular** • vocabulary

| | | | | | |
|---|---|---|---|---|---|
| **der Zug**<br>move | **gewinnen**<br>win (v) | **der Verlierer**<br>loser | **das Bridge**<br>bridge | **der Punkt**<br>point | **Wer ist dran?**<br>Whose turn is it? |
| **spielen**<br>play (v) | **der Gewinner**<br>winner | **das Spiel**<br>game | **das Poker**<br>poker | **die Farbe**<br>suit | **Du bist dran.**<br>It's your move. |
| **der Spieler**<br>player | **verlieren**<br>lose (v) | **die Wette**<br>bet | **das Kartenspiel**<br>deck of cards | **das Spielergebnis**<br>score | **Würfle.**<br>Roll the dice. |

# das Kunsthandwerk 1 • arts and crafts 1

die Künstlerin
artist

das Gemälde
painting

die Staffelei
easel

die Leinwand
canvas

der Pinsel
brush

die Palette
palette

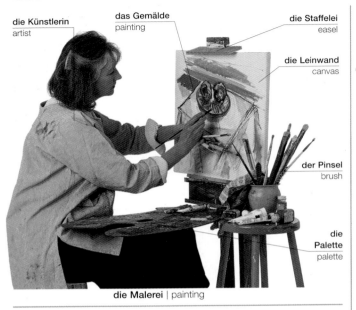
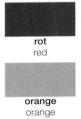

die Malerei | painting

## die Farben • paints

die Ölfarben
oil paint

die Aquarellfarbe
watercolor paint

die Pastellstifte
pastels

die Acrylfarbe
acrylic paint

die Plakatfarbe
poster paint

## die Farben • colors

| | | | |
|---|---|---|---|
| **rot** red | **blau** blue | **gelb** yellow | **grün** green |
| **orange** orange | **lila** purple | **weiß** white | **schwarz** black |
| **grau** gray | **rosa** pink | **braun** brown | **indigoblau** indigo |

# andere Kunstfertigkeiten • other crafts

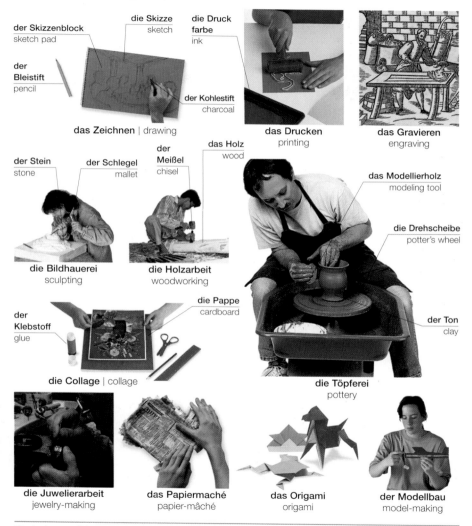

der Skizzenblock
sketch pad

der Bleistift
pencil

die Skizze
sketch

die Druckfarbe
ink

der Kohlestift
charcoal

**das Zeichnen** | drawing

**das Drucken**
printing

**das Gravieren**
engraving

der Stein
stone

der Schlegel
mallet

der Meißel
chisel

das Holz
wood

das Modellierholz
modeling tool

die Drehscheibe
potter's wheel

**die Bildhauerei**
sculpting

**die Holzarbeit**
woodworking

der Ton
clay

der Klebstoff
glue

die Pappe
cardboard

**die Collage** | collage

**die Töpferei**
pottery

**die Juwelierarbeit**
jewelry-making

**das Papiermaché**
papier-mâché

**das Origami**
origami

**der Modellbau**
model-making

# das Kunsthandwerk 2 • arts and crafts 2

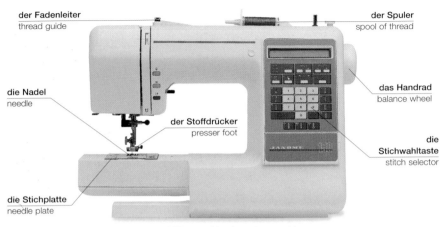

der Fadenleiter
thread guide

der Spuler
spool of thread

die Nadel
needle

das Handrad
balance wheel

der Stoffdrücker
presser foot

die Stichwahltaste
stitch selector

die Stichplatte
needle plate

die **Nähmaschine** | sewing machine

die Schere
scissors

das Schnittmuster
pattern

das Nadelkissen
pincushion

die Stecknadel
pin

das Zentimetermaß
tape measure

der Stoff
material

der **Nähkorb** | sewing basket

das Garn
thread

die Öse
eye

die Spule
bobbin

der Haken
hook

der Fingerhut
thimble

die
Schneiderkreide
tailor's chalk

die
Schneiderpuppe
tailor's dummy

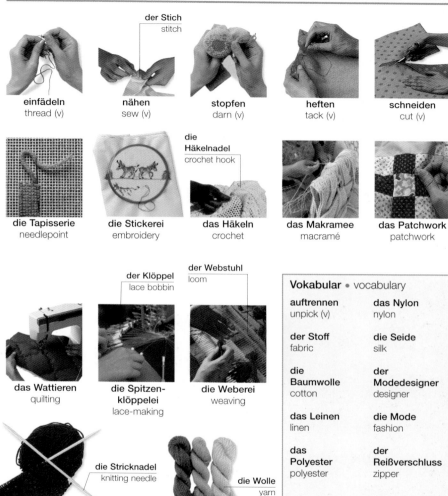

**einfädeln**
thread (v)

**der Stich**
stitch

**nähen**
sew (v)

**stopfen**
darn (v)

**heften**
tack (v)

**schneiden**
cut (v)

**die Tapisserie**
needlepoint

**die Stickerei**
embroidery

**die Häkelnadel**
crochet hook

**das Häkeln**
crochet

**das Makramee**
macramé

**das Patchwork**
patchwork

**das Wattieren**
quilting

**der Klöppel**
lace bobbin

**die Spitzen-klöppelei**
lace-making

**der Webstuhl**
loom

**die Weberei**
weaving

**das Stricken** | knitting

**die Stricknadel**
knitting needle

**die Wolle**
yarn

**der Strang** | skein

**Vokabular** • vocabulary

**auftrennen**
unpick (v)

**das Nylon**
nylon

**der Stoff**
fabric

**die Seide**
silk

**die Baumwolle**
cotton

**der Modedesigner**
designer

**das Leinen**
linen

**die Mode**
fashion

**das Polyester**
polyester

**der Reißverschluss**
zipper

**die Umwelt**
environment

# der Weltraum • space

der Merkur
Mercury

die Erde
Earth

der Mars
Mars

der Jupiter
Jupiter

der Neptun
Neptune

der Uranus
Uranus

der Pluto
Pluto

die Venus
Venus

die Sonne
Sun

der Mond
Moon

der Saturn
Saturn

**das Sonnensystem** | solar system

der Schweif
tail

der Stern
star

**die Galaxie**
galaxy

**der Nebelfleck**
nebula

**der Asteroid**
asteroid

**der Komet**
comet

**vokabular** • vocabulary

| | | |
|---|---|---|
| **der Planet**<br>planet | **das Universum**<br>universe | **der Vollmond**<br>full moon |
| **der Meteor**<br>meteor | **die Umlaufbahn**<br>orbit | **der Neumond**<br>new moon |
| **die Schwerkraft**<br>gravity | **das schwarze Loch**<br>black hole | **die Mondsichel**<br>crescent moon |

**die Finsternis** | eclipse

# die Raumforschung • space exploration

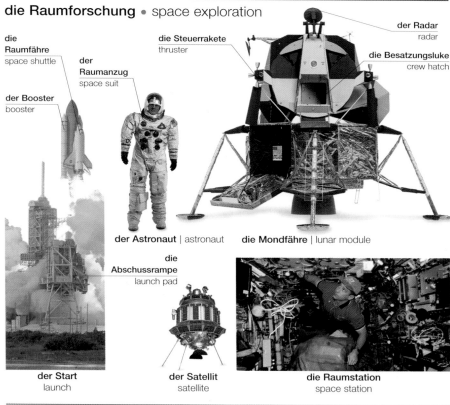

**der Radar**
radar

**die Steuerrakete**
thruster

**die Besatzungsluke**
crew hatch

**die Raumfähre**
space shuttle

**der Raumanzug**
space suit

**der Booster**
booster

**der Astronaut** | astronaut

**die Mondfähre** | lunar module

**der Start**
launch

**die Abschussrampe**
launch pad

**der Satellit**
satellite

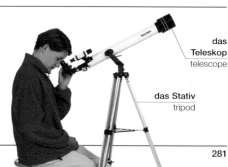

**die Raumstation**
space station

# die Astronomie • astronomy

**das Sternbild**
constellation

**das Fernglas**
binoculars

**das Teleskop**
telescope

**das Stativ**
tripod

# die Erde • Earth

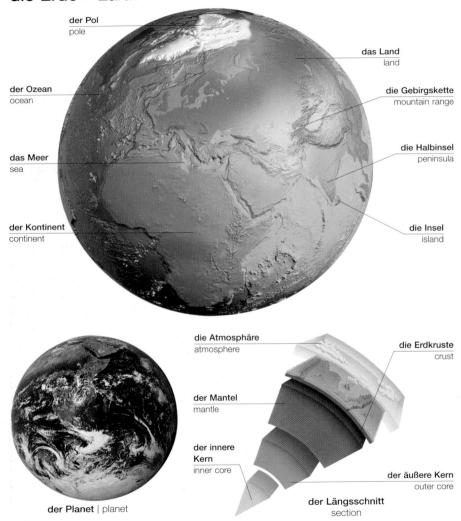

**der Pol**
pole

**das Land**
land

**der Ozean**
ocean

**die Gebirgskette**
mountain range

**die Halbinsel**
peninsula

**das Meer**
sea

**der Kontinent**
continent

**die Insel**
island

**die Atmosphäre**
atmosphere

**die Erdkruste**
crust

**der Mantel**
mantle

**der innere Kern**
inner core

**der äußere Kern**
outer core

**der Planet** | planet

**der Längsschnitt**
section

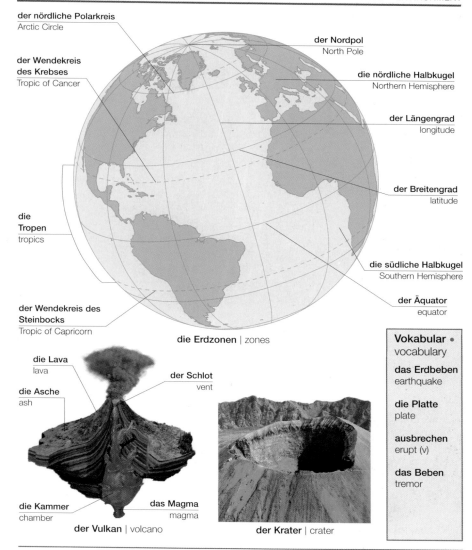

der nördliche Polarkreis
Arctic Circle

der Nordpol
North Pole

der Wendekreis
des Krebses
Tropic of Cancer

die nördliche Halbkugel
Northern Hemisphere

der Längengrad
longitude

der Breitengrad
latitude

die
Tropen
tropics

die südliche Halbkugel
Southern Hemisphere

der Äquator
equator

der Wendekreis des
Steinbocks
Tropic of Capricorn

**die Erdzonen** | zones

die Lava
lava

der Schlot
vent

die Asche
ash

**Vokabular** •
vocabulary

**das Erdbeben**
earthquake

**die Platte**
plate

**ausbrechen**
erupt (v)

**das Beben**
tremor

die Kammer
chamber

das Magma
magma

**der Vulkan** | volcano

**der Krater** | crater

# die Landschaft • landscape

**der Berg**
mountain

**der Hang**
slope

**das Ufer**
bank

**der Fluss**
river

**die Strom schnellen**
rapids

**die Felsen**
rocks

**der Gletscher**
glacier

**das Tal** | valley

**der Hügel**
hill

**das Plateau**
plateau

**die Schlucht**
gorge

**die Höhle**
cave

**die Ebene** | plain

**die Wüste** | desert

**der Wald** | forest

**der Wald** | woods

**der Regenwald**
rain forest

**der Sumpf**
swamp

**die Wiese label**
meadow

**das Grasland**
grassland

**der Wasserfall**
waterfall

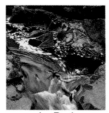

**der Bach**
stream

**der See**
lake

**der Geysir**
geyser

**die Küste**
coast

**die Klippe**
cliff

**das Korallenriff**
coral reef

**die Flussmündung**
estuary

# das Wetter • weather

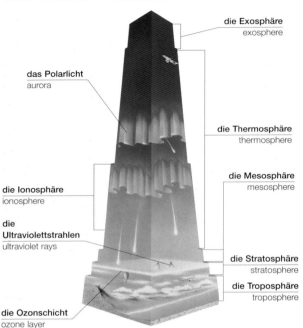

die Exosphäre
exosphere

das Polarlicht
aurora

die Thermosphäre
thermosphere

die Mesosphäre
mesosphere

die Ionosphäre
ionosphere

die
Ultraviolettstrahlen
ultraviolet rays

die Stratosphäre
stratosphere

die Troposphäre
troposphere

die Ozonschicht
ozone layer

**die Atmosphäre** | atmosphere

**der Sonnenschein**
sunshine

**der Wind**
wind

## Vokabular • vocabulary

| | | | | | |
|---|---|---|---|---|---|
| **der Schneeregen**<br>sleet | **der Schauer**<br>shower | **heiß**<br>hot | **trocken**<br>dry | **windig**<br>windy | **Mir ist heiß/kalt.**<br>I'm hot/cold. |
| **der Hagel**<br>hail | **sonnig**<br>sunny | **kalt**<br>cold | **nass**<br>wet | **der Sturm**<br>gale | **Es regnet.**<br>It's raining. |
| **der Donner**<br>thunder | **bewölkt**<br>cloudy | **warm**<br>warm | **feucht**<br>humid | **die Temperatur**<br>temperature | **Es sind…Grad.**<br>It's…degrees. |

**die Wolke**
cloud

**der Regen**
rain

**der Blitz**
lightning

**das Gewitter**
storm

**der feine Nebel**
mist

**der dichte Nebel**
fog

**der Regenbogen**
rainbow

**der Schnee**
snow

**der Raureif**
frost

**der Eiszapfen**
icicle

**das Eis**
ice

**der Frost**
freeze

**der Hurrikan**
hurricane

**der Tornado**
tornado

**der Monsun**
monsoon

**die Überschwemmung**
flood

# das Gestein • rocks

## eruptiv • igneous

**der Granit**
granite

**der Obsidian**
obsidian

**der Basalt**
basalt

**der Bimsstein**
pumice

## sedimentär • sedimentary

**der Sandstein**
sandstone

**der Kalkstein**
limestone

**die Kreide**
chalk

**der Feuerstein**
flint

**das Konglomerat**
conglomerate

**die Kohle**
coal

## metamorph • metamorphic

**der Schiefer**
slate

**der Glimmers**
schist

**der Gneis**
gneiss

**der Marmor**
marble

## die Schmucksteine • gems

**der Rubin**
ruby

**der Amethyst**
amethyst

**der Diamant**
diamond

**der Jett**
jet

**der Opal**
opal

**der Mondstein**
moonstone

**der Granat**
garnet

**der Topas**
topaz

**der Aquamarin**
aquamarine

**der Jade**
jade

**der Smaragd**
emerald

**der Saphir**
sapphire

**der Turmalin**
tourmaline

# die Mineralien • minerals

| **der Quarz**<br>quartz | **der Glimmer**<br>mica | **der Schwefel**<br>sulfur | **der Hämatit**<br>hematite | **der Kalzit**<br>calcite |

| **der Malachit**<br>malachite | **der Türkis**<br>turquoise | **der Onyx**<br>onyx | **der Achat**<br>agate | **der Graphit**<br>graphite |

# die Metalle • metals

| **das Gold**<br>gold | **das Silber**<br>silver | **das Platin**<br>platinum | **das Nickel**<br>nickel | **das Eisen**<br>iron |

| **das Kupfer**<br>copper | **das Zinn**<br>tin | **das Aluminium**<br>aluminum | **das Quecksilber**<br>mercury | **das Zink**<br>zinc |

# die Tiere 1 • animals 1
## die Säugetiere • mammals

die Schnurrhaare
whiskers

der Schwanz
tail

**das Kaninchen**
rabbit

**der Hamster**
hamster

**die Maus**
mouse

**die Ratte**
rat

**der Igel**
hedgehog

**das Eichhörnchen**
squirrel

**die Fledermaus**
bat

**der Waschbär**
raccoon

**der Fuchs**
fox

**der Wolf**
wolf

der Welpe
puppy

das Kätzchen
kitten

das Junge
pup

**der Hund**
dog

**die Katze**
cat

**der Otter**
otter

**die Robbe**
seal

die Flosse
flipper

das Atemloch
blowhole

**der Seelöwe**
sea lion

**das Walross**
walrus

**der Wal**
whale

**der Delphin**
dolphin

das Geweih
antler

die Mähne
mane

der Höcker
hump

der Huf
hoof

**der Hirsch**
deer

**das Zebra**
zebra

**die Giraffe**
giraffe

**das Kamel**
camel

der Rüssel
trunk

der Stoßzahn
tusk

das Horn
horn

**das Nilpferd**
hippopotamus

**der Elefant**
elephant

**das Nashorn**
rhinoceros

**der Tiger**
tiger

die Mähne
mane

**der Löwe**
lion

**der Affe**
monkey

**der Gorilla**
gorilla

**der Koalabär**
koala

der Beutel
pouch

**der Pandabär**
panda

die Klaue
claw

**das Känguru**
kangaroo

**der Bär**
bear

**der Eisbär**
polar bear

**deutsch** • english

# die Tiere 2 • animals 2
## die Vögel • birds

der Schwanz
tail

**der Kanarienvogel**
canary

**der Spatz**
sparrow

**der Kolibri**
hummingbird

**die Schwalbe**
swallow

**die Krähe**
crow

**die Taube**
pigeon

**der Specht**
woodpecker

**der Falke**
falcon

**die Eule**
owl

**die Möwe**
gull

**der Adler**
eagle

**der Pelikan**
pelican

**der Flamingo**
flamingo

**der Storch**
stork

**der Kranich**
crane

**der Pinguin**
penguin

**der Strauß**
ostrich

## die Reptilien • reptiles

die Gans | goose

der Schwan
swan

der Pfau
peacock

der Fasan
pheasant

der Truthahn
turkey

der Kakadu
cockatoo

der Schnabel
beak

die Feder
feather

der Flügel
wing

die Kralle
claw

der Papagei
parrot

die Schuppen
scales

der Alligator
alligator

die Eidechse
lizard

der Leguan
iguana

der Panzer
shell

die Wasserschildkröte
turtle

die Schildkröte
tortoise

die Schlange
snake

die Schnauze
snout

das Krokodil
crocodile

# die Tiere 3 • animals 3
## die Amphibien • amphibians

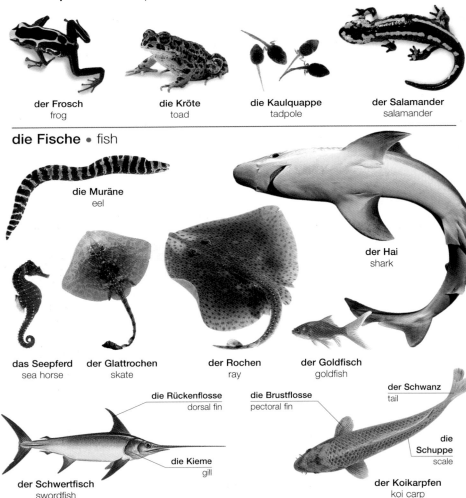

**der Frosch**
frog

**die Kröte**
toad

**die Kaulquappe**
tadpole

**der Salamander**
salamander

## die Fische • fish

**die Muräne**
eel

**der Hai**
shark

**das Seepferd**
sea horse

**der Glattrochen**
skate

**der Rochen**
ray

**der Goldfisch**
goldfish

**die Rückenflosse**
dorsal fin

**die Brustflosse**
pectoral fin

**der Schwanz**
tail

**die Kieme**
gill

**die Schuppe**
scale

**der Schwertfisch**
swordfish

**der Koikarpfen**
koi carp

# die Wirbellosen • invertebrates

**die Ameise**
ant

**die Termite**
termite

**die Biene**
bee

**die Wespe**
wasp

**der Käfer**
beetle

**der Kakerlak**
cockroach

**die Motte**
moth

**der Schmetterling**
butterfly

**der Fühler**
antenna

**der Kokon**
cocoon

**die Raupe**
caterpillar

**die Grille**
cricket

**die Heuschrecke**
grasshopper

**die Gottesanbeterin**
praying mantis

**der Stachel**
sting

**der Skorpion**
scorpion

**der Tausendfüßer**
centipede

**die Libelle**
dragonfly

**die Fliege**
fly

**die Stechmücke**
mosquito

**der Marienkäfer**
ladybug

**die Spinne**
spider

**die Wegschnecke**
slug

**die Schnecke**
snail

**der Wurm**
worm

**der Seestern**
starfish

**die Muschel**
mussel

**der Krebs**
crab

**der Hummer**
lobster

**der Krake**
octopus

**der Tintenfisch**
squid

**die Qualle**
jellyfish

# die Pflanzen • plants

## der Baum • tree

der Ast
branch

das Blatt
leaf

der Zweig
twig

die Rinde
bark

die Weide
willow

die Wurzel
root

der Stamm
trunk

**die Eiche**
oak

**die Pappel**
poplar

**der Eukalyptus**
eucalyptus

**die Lärche**
larch

**die Buche**
beech

**die Birke**
birch

**die Kiefer**
pine

**die Zeder**
cedar

**der Ahorn**
maple

**die Ulme**
elm

**die Linde**
lime

**die Stechpalme**
holly

die Beere
berry

**die Palme**
palm

# die blühende Pflanze • flowering plant

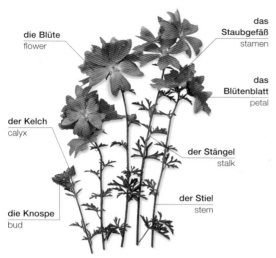

die Blüte
flower

das
Staubgefäß
stamen

das
Blütenblatt
petal

der Kelch
calyx

der Stängel
stalk

der Stiel
stem

die Knospe
bud

**der Hahnenfuß**
buttercup

**das
Gänseblümchen**
daisy

**die Distel**
thistle

**der Löwenzahn**
dandelion

**das Heidekraut**
heather

**der
Klatschmohn**
poppy

**der Fingerhut**
foxglove

**das Geißblatt**
honeysuckle

**die
Sonnenblume**
sunflower

**der Klee**
clover

**die
Sternhyazinthen**
bluebells

**die
Schlüsselblume**
primrose

**die Lupinen**
lupines

**die Nessel**
nettle

# die Stadt • town

die Straße
street

die
Bordsteinkante
curb

die Straßenecke
street corner

der Laden
store

die Kreuzung
intersection

die Einbahn
straße
one-way
system

der
Bürgersteig
sidewalk

das
Bürogebäude
office building

der
Wohnblock
apartment
building

die Gasse
alley

der Parkplatz
parking lot

das Straßenschild
street sign

der Poller
barrier

die Straßenlaterne
streetlight

# die Gebäude • buildings

**das Rathaus**
town hall

**die Bibliothek**
library

**das Kino**
movie theater

**das Theater**
theater

**die Universität**
university

**der Wolkenkratzer**
skyscraper

## die Wohngegend • areas

**das Industriegebiet**
industrial park

**die Stadt**
city

**der Vorort**
suburb

**das Dorf**
village

**die Schule**
school

## Vokabular • vocabulary

| | | | | |
|---|---|---|---|---|
| **die Fußgängerzone**<br>pedestrian zone | **die Seitenstraße**<br>side street | **der Kanalschacht**<br>manhole | **der Rinnstein**<br>gutter | **die Kirche**<br>church |
| **die Allee**<br>avenue | **der Platz**<br>square | **die Bushaltestelle**<br>bus stop | **die Fabrik**<br>factory | **der Kanal**<br>drain |

---

# die Architektur • architecture

## die Gebäude und Strukturen • buildings and structures

**der Mauerturm**
turret

**der Burggraben**
moat

**der Wolkenkratzer**
skyscraper

**die Burg**
castle

**die Kuppel**
dome

**der Turm**
tower

**die Kirche**
church

**die Moschee**
mosque

**das Gewölbe**
vault

**das Gesims**
cornice

**der Tempel**
temple

**die Synagoge**
synagogue

**die Säule**
pillar

**der Staudamm**
dam

**die Brücke**
bridge

die
**Kreuzblume**
finial

die
**Turmspitze**
spire

**der Giebel**
gable

**die Kathedrale** | cathedral

# die Baustile • styles

**gotisch**
Gothic

der Architrav
architrave

**die Renaissance**
Renaissance

**barock**
Baroque

der Bogen
arch

der Fries
frieze

der Chor
choir

**das Rokoko**
Rococo

das Giebeldreieck
pediment

der Strebepfeiler
buttress

**klassizistisch**
Neoclassical

**der Jugendstil**
Art Nouveau

**das Art-déco**
Art Deco

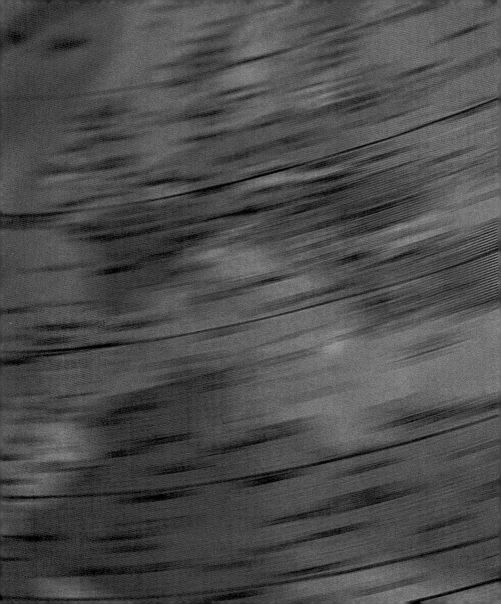

**die Information**
reference

# die Uhrzeit • time

der Minutenzeiger
minute hand

der Stundenzeiger
hour hand

die Uhr
clock

**Vokabular** • vocabulary

| | | |
|---|---|---|
| **die Stunde**<br>hour | **jetzt**<br>now | **zwanzig Minuten**<br>twenty minutes |
| **die Minute**<br>minute | **später**<br>later | **vierzig Minuten**<br>forty minutes |
| **die Sekunde**<br>second | **eine halbe stunde**<br>half an hour | **eine Viertelstunde**<br>a quarter of an hour |

**Wie spät ist es?**
What time is it?

**Es ist drei Uhr.**
It's three o'clock.

**fünf nach eins**
five past one

**zehn nach eins**
ten past one

**Viertel nach eins**
quarter past one

**zwanzig nach eins**
twenty past one

der
Sekundenzeiger
second hand

**fünf vor halb zwei**
twenty-five past one

**ein Uhr dreißig**
one thirty

**fünf nach halb zwei**
twenty-five to two

**zwanzig vor zwei**
twenty to two

**Viertel vor zwei**
quarter to two

**zehn vor zwei**
ten to two

**fünf vor zwei**
five to two

**zwei Uhr**
two o'clock

deutsch • english

# die Nacht und der Tag • night and day

**die Mitternacht**
midnight

**der Sonnenaufgang**
sunrise

**die Morgendämmerung**
dawn

**der Morgen**
morning

**der Sonnenuntergang**
sunset

**der Mittag**
noon

**die Abenddämmerung**
dusk

**der Abend**
evening

**der Nachmittag**
afternoon

## Vokabular • vocabulary

| | | | |
|---|---|---|---|
| **früh**<br>early | **Du bist früh.**<br>You're early. | **Sei bitte pünktlich.**<br>Please be on time. | **Wann ist es zu Ende?**<br>What time does it end? |
| **pünktlich**<br>on time | **Du hast dich verspätet.**<br>You're late. | **Bis später.**<br>I'll see you later. | **Wie lange dauert es?**<br>How long will it last? |
| **spät**<br>late | **Ich werde bald dort sein.**<br>I'll be there soon. | **Wann fängt es an?**<br>What time does it start? | **Es ist schon spät.**<br>It's getting late. |

# der Kalender • calendar

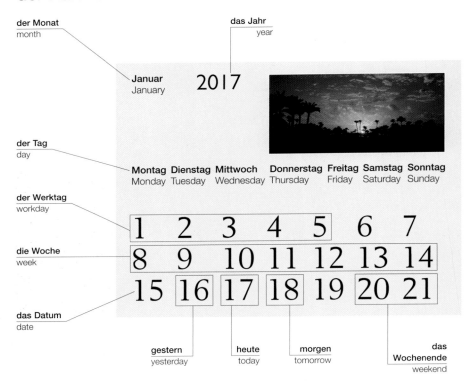

**der Monat**
month

**das Jahr**
year

**Januar**
January

2017

**der Tag**
day

**der Werktag**
workday

**die Woche**
week

**das Datum**
date

| **Montag** | **Dienstag** | **Mittwoch** | **Donnerstag** | **Freitag** | **Samstag** | **Sonntag** |
|---|---|---|---|---|---|---|
| Monday | Tuesday | Wednesday | Thursday | Friday | Saturday | Sunday |
| 1 | 2 | 3 | 4 | 5 | 6 | 7 |
| 8 | 9 | 10 | 11 | 12 | 13 | 14 |
| 15 | 16 | 17 | 18 | 19 | 20 | 21 |

**gestern**
yesterday

**heute**
today

**morgen**
tomorrow

**das Wochenende**
weekend

**Vokabular** • vocabulary

| **Januar** | **März** | **Mai** | **Juli** | **September** | **November** |
|---|---|---|---|---|---|
| January | March | May | July | September | November |
| **Februar** | **April** | **Juni** | **August** | **Oktober** | **Dezember** |
| February | April | June | August | October | December |

# die Jahre • years

| 1900 | **neunzehnhundert** • nineteen hundred |
| 1901 | **neunzehnhunderteins** • nineteen hundred and one |
| 1910 | **neunzehnhundertzehn** • nineteen ten |
| 2000 | **zweitausend** • two thousand |
| 2001 | **zweitausendeins** • two thousand and one |

## die Jahreszeiten • seasons

**der Frühling**
spring

**der Sommer**
summer

**der Herbst**
fall

**der Winter**
winter

---

**Vokabular** • vocabulary

| | | |
|---|---|---|
| **das Jahrhundert** <br> century | **letzte Woche** <br> last week | **monatlich** <br> monthly |
| **das Jahrzehnt** <br> decade | **nächste Woche** <br> next week | **jährlich** <br> annual |
| **das Jahrtausend** <br> millennium | **vorgestern** <br> the day before yesterday | |
| **vierzehn Tage** <br> two weeks | **übermorgen** <br> the day after tomorrow | **Welches Datum haben wir heute?** <br> What's the date today? |
| **diese Woche** <br> this week | **wöchentlich** <br> weekly | **Heute ist der siebte Februar zweitausendsiebzehn.** <br> It's February seventh, two thousand seventeen. |

---

# die Zahlen • numbers

| | |
|---|---|
| 0 | null • zero |
| 1 | eins • one |
| 2 | zwei • two |
| 3 | drei • three |
| 4 | vier • four |
| 5 | fünf • five |
| 6 | sechs • six |
| 7 | sieben • seven |
| 8 | acht • eight |
| 9 | neun • nine |
| 10 | zehn • ten |
| 11 | elf • eleven |
| 12 | zwölf • twelve |
| 13 | dreizehn • thirteen |
| 14 | vierzehn • fourteen |
| 15 | fünfzehn • fifteen |
| 16 | sechzehn • sixteen |
| 17 | siebzehn • seventeen |
| 18 | achtzehn • eighteen |
| 19 | neunzehn • nineteen |

| | |
|---|---|
| 20 | zwanzig • twenty |
| 21 | einundzwanzig • twenty-one |
| 22 | zweiundzwanzig • twenty-two |
| 30 | dreißig • thirty |
| 40 | vierzig • forty |
| 50 | fünfzig • fifty |
| 60 | sechzig • sixty |
| 70 | siebzig • seventy |
| 80 | achtzig • eighty |
| 90 | neunzig • ninety |
| 100 | hundert • one hundred |
| 110 | hundertzehn • one hundred and ten |
| 200 | zweihundert • two hundred |
| 300 | dreihundert • three hundred |
| 400 | vierhundert • four hundred |
| 500 | fünfhundert • five hundred |
| 600 | sechshundert • six hundred |
| 700 | siebenhundert • seven hundred |
| 800 | achthundert • eight hundred |
| 900 | neunhundert • nine hundred |

deutsch • english

1,000 **tausend** • one thousand

10,000 **zehntausend** • ten thousand

20,000 **zwanzigtausend** • twenty thousand

50,000 **fünfzigtausend** • fifty thousand

55,500 **fünfundfünfzigtausend-fünfhundert** • fifty-five thousand five hundred

100,000 **hunderttausend** • one hundred thousand

1,000,000 **eine Million** • one million

1,000,000,000 **eine Milliarde** • one billion

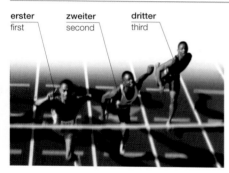

**erster** first
**zweiter** second
**dritter** third

**sechzehnter**
• sixteenth

**siebzehnter**
• seventeenth

**achtzehnter**
• eighteenth

**neunzehnter**
• nineteenth

**zwanzigster**
• twentieth

**einundzwanzigster**
• twenty-first

**zweiundzwanzigster**
• twenty-second

**dreiundzwanzigster**
• twenty-third

**dreißigster**
• thirtieth

**vierzigster**
• fortieth

**fünfzigster**
• fiftieth

**sechzigster**
• sixtieth

**siebzigster**
• seventieth

**achtzigster**
• eightieth

**neunzigster**
• ninetieth

**hundertster**
• (one) hundredth

**vierter** • fourth

**fünfter** • fifth

**sechster** • sixth

**siebter** • seventh

**achter** • eighth

**neunter** • ninth

**zehnter** • tenth

**elfter** • eleventh

**zwölfter** • twelfth

**dreizehnter** • thirteenth

**vierzehnter** • fourteenth

**fünfzehnter** • fifteenth

# die Maße und Gewichte • weights and measures

## die Fläche • area

| der Qua-<br>dratfuß | der Quadrat-<br>meter |
|---|---|
| square<br>foot | square meter |

## die Entfernung • distance

| der<br>Kilometer | die Meile |
|---|---|
| kilometer | mile |

die Waagschale
pan

das Pfund
pound

das Kilogramm
kilogram

die Unze
ounce

das Gramm
gram

die Waage | scale

### Vokabular • vocabulary

| | | |
|---|---|---|
| **das Yard**<br>yard | **die Tonne**<br>ton | **messen**<br>measure (v) |
| **der Meter**<br>meter | **das Milligramm**<br>milligram | **wiegen**<br>weigh (v) |

## die Länge • length

der Fuß
foot

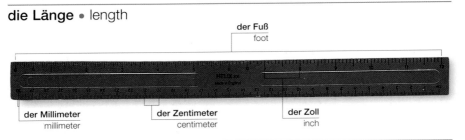

| der Millimeter | der Zentimeter | der Zoll |
|---|---|---|
| millimeter | centimeter | inch |

deutsch • english

# das Fassungsvermögen • capacity

der halbe Liter
half-liter

das Pint
pint

das Volumen
volume

der Milliliter
milliliter

**der Messbecher**
measuring cup

**das Flüssigkeitsmaß**
liquid measure

# der Behälter • container

**die Tüte**
carton

**das Päckchen**
packet

**die Flasche**
bottle

**der Beutel**
bag

**die Dose** | tub

**das Glas** | jar

die Dose
can

**die Dose** | tin

**der Sprühbehälter**
spray bottle

das Stück
bar

**die Tube**
tube

**die Rolle**
roll

**das Päckchen**
pack

**die Sprühdose**
spray can

# die Weltkarte • world map

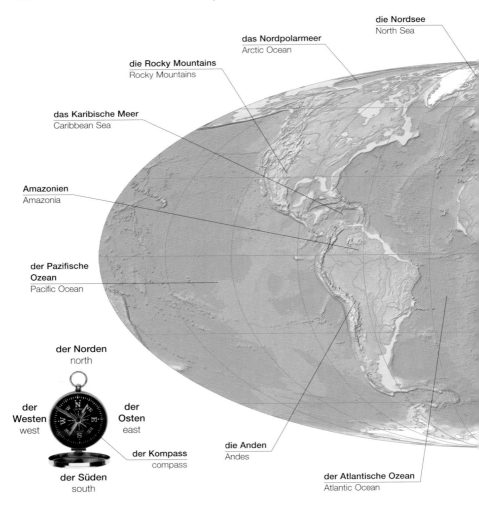

die Nordsee
North Sea

das Nordpolarmeer
Arctic Ocean

die Rocky Mountains
Rocky Mountains

das Karibische Meer
Caribbean Sea

Amazonien
Amazonia

der Pazifische
Ozean
Pacific Ocean

der Norden
north

der
Westen
west

der
Osten
east

der Kompass
compass

der Süden
south

die Anden
Andes

der Atlantische Ozean
Atlantic Ocean

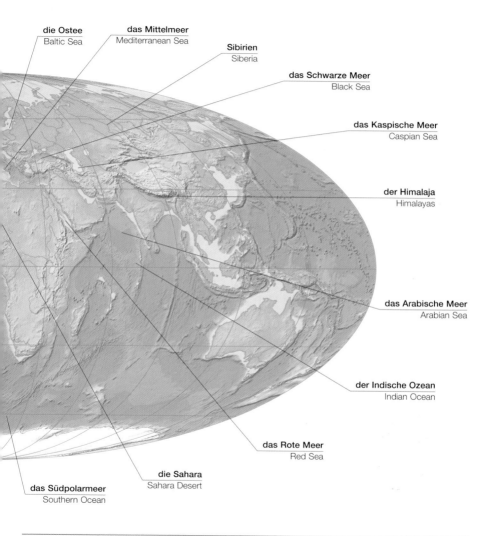

**die Ostee**
Baltic Sea

**das Mittelmeer**
Mediterranean Sea

**Sibirien**
Siberia

**das Schwarze Meer**
Black Sea

**das Kaspische Meer**
Caspian Sea

**der Himalaja**
Himalayas

**das Arabische Meer**
Arabian Sea

**der Indische Ozean**
Indian Ocean

**das Rote Meer**
Red Sea

**die Sahara**
Sahara Desert

**das Südpolarmeer**
Southern Ocean

**deutsch** • english

# Nord- und Mittelamerika • North and Central America

**Hawaii**
Hawaii

1 **Alaska** • Alaska
2 **Kanada** • Canada
3 **Grönland** • Greenland
4 **die Vereinigten Staaten** •
United States of America
5 **Mexiko** • Mexico
6 **Guatemala** • Guatemala
7 **Belize** • Belize
8 **El Salvador** • El Salvador
9 **Honduras** • Honduras
10 **Nicaragua** • Nicaragua
11 **Costa Rica** • Costa Rica
12 **Panama** • Panama
13 **Kuba** • Cuba
14 **die Bahamas** • Bahamas
15 **Jamaika** • Jamaica
16 **Haiti** • Haiti
17 **die Dominikanische Republik** •
Dominican Republic
18 **Puerto Rico** • Puerto Rico
19 **Barbados** • Barbados
20 **Trinidad und Tobago** • Trinidad and Tobago
21 **Saint Kitts und Nevis** • St. Kitts and Nevis

22 **Antigua und Barbuda** • Antigua and Barbuda
23 **Dominica** • Dominica
24 **Saint Lucia** • St. Lucia
25 **Saint Vinzent und die Grenadinen** •
St. Vincent and The Grenadines
26 **Grenada** • Grenada

# Südamerika • South America

1 **Venezuela** • Venezuela
2 **Kolumbien** • Colombia
3 **Ecuador** • Ecuador
4 **Peru** • Peru
5 **die Galapagosinseln** •
   Galápagos Islands
6 **Guyana** • Guyana
7 **Suriname** • Suriname
8 **Französisch-Guayana** •
   French Guiana
9 **Brasilien** • Brazil
10 **Bolivien** • Bolivia
11 **Chile** • Chile
12 **Argentinien** • Argentina
13 **Paraguay** • Paraguay
14 **Uruguay** • Uruguay
15 **die Falklandinseln** •
   Falkland Islands

## Vokabular • vocabulary

| | | |
|---|---|---|
| **der Staat** state | **die Kolonie** colony | **die Zone** zone |
| **das Land** country | **die Provinz** province | **die Region** region |
| **die Nation** nation | **das Territorium** territory | **der Bezirk** district |
| **der Kontinent** continent | **das Fürstentum** principality | **die Hauptstadt** capital |

# Europa • Europe

1 **Irland** • Ireland

2 **das Vereinigte Königreich** • United Kingdom

3 **Portugal** • Portugal

4 **Spanien** • Spain

5 **die Balearen** • Balearic Islands

6 **Andorra** • Andorra

7 **Frankreich** • France

8 **Belgien** • Belgium

9 **die Niederlande** • Netherlands

10 **Luxemburg** • Luxembourg

11 **Deutschland** • Germany

12 **Dänemark** • Denmark

13 **Norwegen** • Norway

14 **Schweden** • Sweden

15 **Finnland** • Finland

16 **Estland** • Estonia

17 **Lettland** • Latvia

18 **Litauen** • Lithuania

19 **Kaliningrad** • Kaliningrad

20 **Polen** • Poland

21 **die Tschechische Republik** • Czech Republic

22 **Österreich** • Austria

23 **Liechtenstein** • Liechtenstein

24 **die Schweiz** • Switzerland

25 **Italien** • Italy

26 **Monaco** • Monaco

27 **Korsika** • Corsica

28 **Sardinien** • Sardinia

29 **San Marino** • San Marino

30 **die Vatikanstadt** • Vatican City

31 **Sizilien** • Sicily

32 **Malta** • Malta

33 **Slowenien** • Slovenia

34 **Kroatien** • Croatia

35 **Ungarn** • Hungary

36 **die Slowakei** • Slovakia

37 **die Ukraine** • Ukraine

38 **Weißrussland** • Belarus

39 **Moldawien** • Moldova

40 **Rumänien** • Romania

41 **Serbien** • Serbia

42 **Bosnien und Herzegowina** • Bosnia and Herzegovina

43 **Albanien** • Albania

44 **Mazedonien** • Macedonia

45 **Bulgarien** • Bulgaria

46 **Griechenland** • Greece

47 **Kosovo** • Kosovo

48 **Montenegro** • Montenegro

49 **Island** • Iceland

# Afrika • Africa

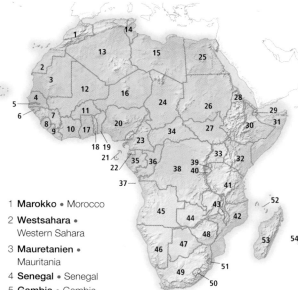

1 **Marokko** • Morocco

2 **Westsahara** • Western Sahara

3 **Mauretanien** • Mauritania

4 **Senegal** • Senegal

5 **Gambia** • Gambia

6 **Guinea-Bissau** • Guinea-Bissau

7 **Guinea** • Guinea

8 **Sierra Leone** • Sierra Leone

9 **Liberia** • Liberia

10 **Elfenbeinküste** • Ivory Coast

11 **Burkina Faso** • Burkina Faso

12 **Mali** • Mali

13 **Algerien** • Algeria

14 **Tunesien** • Tunisia

15 **Libyen** • Libya

16 **Niger** • Niger

17 **Ghana** • Ghana

18 **Togo** • Togo

19 **Benin** • Benin

20 **Nigeria** • Nigeria

21 **São Tomé und Príncipe** • São Tomé and Principe

22 **Äquatorialguinea** • Equatorial Guinea

23 **Kamerun** • Cameroon

24 **Tschad** • Chad

25 **Ägypten** • Egypt

26 **der Sudan** • Sudan

27 **Südsudan** • South Sudan

28 **Eritrea** • Eritrea

29 **Dschibuti** • Djibouti

30 **Äthiopien** • Ethiopia

31 **Somalia** • Somalia

32 **Kenia** • Kenya

33 **Uganda** • Uganda

34 **die Zentralafrikanische Republik** • Central African Republic

35 **Gabun** • Gabon

36 **Kongo** • Congo

37 **Kabinda** • Cabinda

38 **die Demokratische Republik Kongo** • Democratic Republic of the Congo

39 **Ruanda** • Rwanda

40 **Burundi** • Burundi

41 **Tansania** • Tanzania

42 **Mosambik** • Mozambique

43 **Malawi** • Malawi

44 **Sambia** • Zambia

45 **Angola** • Angola

46 **Namibia** • Namibia

47 **Botsuana** • Botswana

48 **Simbabwe** • Zimbabwe

49 **Südafrika** • South Africa

50 **Lesotho** • Lesotho

51 **Swasiland** • Swaziland

52 **die Komoren** • Comoros

53 **Madagaskar** • Madagascar

54 **Mauritius** • Mauritius

# Asien • Asia

1 **die Türkei** • Turkey
2 **Zypern** • Cyprus
3 **die Russische Föderation** •
  Russian Federation
4 **Georgien** • Georgia
5 **Armenien** • Armenia
6 **Aserbaidschan** • Azerbaijan
7 **der Iran** • Iran
8 **der Irak** • Iraq
9 **Syrien** • Syria
10 **der Libanon** • Lebanon
11 **Israel** • Israel
12 **Jordanien** • Jordan
13 **Saudi-Arabien** •
  Saudi Arabia
14 **Kuwait** • Kuwait
15 **Bahrain** • Bahrain
16 **Katar** • Qatar
17 **Vereinigte Arabische Emirate** •
  United Arab Emirates
18 **Oman** • Oman
19 **der Jemen** • Yemen
20 **Kasachstan** • Kazakhstan
21 **Usbekistan** • Uzbekistan
22 **Turkmenistan** • Turkmenistan
23 **Afghanistan** • Afghanistan
24 **Tadschikistan** • Tajikistan
25 **Kirgisistan** • Kyrgyzstan
26 **Pakistan** • Pakistan
27 **Indien** • India
28 **die Malediven** • Maldives
29 **Sri Lanka** • Sri Lanka
30 **China** • China
31 **die Mongolei** • Mongolia
32 **Nordkorea** • North Korea
33 **Südkorea** • South Korea
34 **Japan** • Japan

35 **Nepal** • Nepal
36 **Bhutan** • Bhutan
37 **Bangladesch** • Bangladesh
38 **Myanmar (Birma)** •
  Myanmar (Burma)
39 **Thailand** • Thailand
40 **Laos** • Laos
41 **Vietnam** • Vietnam

deutsch • english

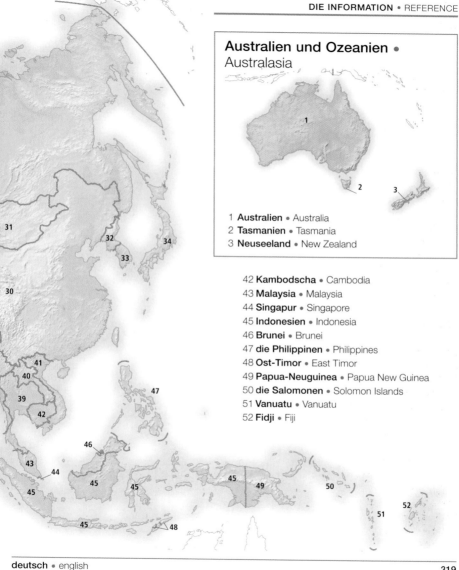

## Australien und Ozeanien •
## Australasia

1 **Australien** • Australia
2 **Tasmanien** • Tasmania
3 **Neuseeland** • New Zealand

42 **Kambodscha** • Cambodia
43 **Malaysia** • Malaysia
44 **Singapur** • Singapore
45 **Indonesien** • Indonesia
46 **Brunei** • Brunei
47 **die Philippinen** • Philippines
48 **Ost-Timor** • East Timor
49 **Papua-Neuguinea** • Papua New Guinea
50 **die Salomonen** • Solomon Islands
51 **Vanuatu** • Vanuatu
52 **Fidji** • Fiji

# Partikeln und Antonyme • particles and antonyms

| | | | |
|---|---|---|---|
| **zu, nach** <br> to | **von, aus** <br> from | **für** <br> for | **zu** <br> toward |
| **über** <br> over | **unter** <br> under | **entlang** <br> along | **über** <br> across |
| **vor** <br> in front of | **hinter** <br> behind | **mit** <br> with | **ohne** <br> without |
| **auf** <br> onto | **in** <br> into | **vor** <br> before | **nach** <br> after |
| **in** <br> in | **aus** <br> out | **bis** <br> by | **bis** <br> until |
| **über** <br> above | **unter** <br> below | **früh** <br> early | **spät** <br> late |
| **innerhalb** <br> inside | **außerhalb** <br> outside | **jetzt** <br> now | **später** <br> later |
| **hinauf** <br> up | **hinunter** <br> down | **immer** <br> always | **nie** <br> never |
| **an, bei** <br> at | **jenseits** <br> beyond | **oft** <br> often | **selten** <br> rarely |
| **durch** <br> through | **um** <br> around | **gestern** <br> yesterday | **morgen** <br> tomorrow |
| **auf** <br> on top of | **neben** <br> beside | **erste** <br> first | **letzte** <br> last |
| **zwischen** <br> between | **gegenüber** <br> opposite | **jede** <br> every | **etwas** <br> some |
| **nahe** <br> near | **weit** <br> far | **gegen** <br> about | **genau** <br> exactly |
| **hier** <br> here | **dort** <br> there | **ein wenig** <br> a little | **viel** <br> a lot |

| | | | |
|---|---|---|---|
| **groß**<br>large | **klein**<br>small | **heiß**<br>hot | **kalt**<br>cold |
| **breit**<br>wide | **schmal**<br>narrow | **offen**<br>open | **geschlossen**<br>closed |
| **groß**<br>tall | **kurz**<br>short | **voll**<br>full | **leer**<br>empty |
| **hoch**<br>high | **niedrig**<br>low | **neu**<br>new | **alt**<br>old |
| **dick**<br>thick | **dünn**<br>thin | **hell**<br>light | **dunkel**<br>dark |
| **leicht**<br>light | **schwer**<br>heavy | **leicht**<br>easy | **schwer**<br>difficult |
| **hart**<br>hard | **weich**<br>soft | **frei**<br>free | **besetzt**<br>occupied |
| **nass**<br>wet | **trocken**<br>dry | **stark**<br>strong | **schwach**<br>weak |
| **gut**<br>good | **schlecht**<br>bad | **dick**<br>fat | **dünn**<br>thin |
| **schnell**<br>fast | **langsam**<br>slow | **jung**<br>young | **alt**<br>old |
| **richtig**<br>correct | **falsch**<br>wrong | **besser**<br>better | **schlechter**<br>worse |
| **sauber**<br>clean | **schmutzig**<br>dirty | **schwarz**<br>black | **weiß**<br>white |
| **schön**<br>beautiful | **hässlich**<br>ugly | **interessant**<br>interesting | **langweilig**<br>boring |
| **teuer**<br>expensive | **billig**<br>cheap | **krank**<br>sick | **wohl**<br>well |
| **leise**<br>quiet | **laut**<br>noisy | **der Anfang**<br>beginning | **das Ende**<br>end |

# praktische Redewendungen • useful phrases

**wesentliche Redewendungen •**
essential phrases

**Ja**
Yes

**Nein**
No

**Vielleicht**
Maybe

**Bitte**
Please

**Danke**
Thank you

**Bitte sehr**
You're welcome

**Entschuldigung**
Excuse me

**Es tut mir Leid**
I'm sorry

**Nicht**
Don't

**Okay**
OK

**In Ordnung**
That's fine

**Das ist richtig**
That's correct

**Das ist falsch**
That's wrong

**Begrüßungen •**
greetings

**Guten Tag**
Hello

**Auf Wiedersehen**
Goodbye

**Guten Morgen**
Good morning

**Guten Tag**
Good afternoon

**Guten Abend**
Good evening

**Gute Nacht**
Good night

**Wie geht es Ihnen?**
How are you?

**Ich heiße…**
My name is…

**Wie heißen Sie?**
What is your name?

**Wie heißt er/sie?**
What is his/her name?

**Darf ich…vorstellen**
May I introduce…

**Das ist…**
This is…

**Angenehm**
Pleased to meet you

**Bis später**
See you later

**Schilder • signs**

**Touristen-Information**
Tourist information

**Eingang**
Entrance

**Ausgang**
Exit

**Notausgang**
Emergency exit

**Drücken**
Push

**Lebensgefahr**
Danger

**Rauchen verboten**
No smoking

**Außer Betrieb**
Out of order

**Öffnungszeiten**
Opening times

**Eintritt frei**
Free admission

**Reduziert**
Reduced

**Ausverkauf**
Sale

**Bitte anklopfen**
Knock before entering

**Betreten des Rasens verboten**
Keep off the grass

**Hilfe • help**

**Können Sie mir helfen?**
Can you help me?

**Ich verstehe nicht**
I don't understand

**Ich weiß nicht**
I don't know

**Sprechen Sie Englisch?**
Do you speak English?

**Ich spreche Englisch**
I speak English

**Sprechen Sie bitte langsamer**
Please speak more slowly

**Schreiben Sie es bitte für mich auf**
Please write it down for me

**Ich habe… verloren**
I have lost…

**Richtungsangaben • directions**

**Ich habe mich verlaufen**
I am lost

**Wo ist der/die/das...?**
Where is the...?

**Wo ist der/die/das nächste...?**
Where is the nearest...?

**Wo sind die Toiletten?**
Where is the restroom?

**Wie komme ich nach...?**
How do I get to...?

**Nach rechts**
To the right

**Nach links**
To the left

**Geradeaus**
Straight ahead

**Wie weit ist...?**
How far is...?

**die Verkehrsschilder**
• road signs

**Langsam fahren**
Slow down

**Achtung**
Caution

**Keine Zufahrt**
Do not enter

**Umleitung**
Detour

**Rechts fahren**
Keep right

**Autobahn**
Freeway

**Parkverbot**
No parking

**Sackgasse**
Dead end

**Einbahnstraße**
One-way street

**Vorfahrt gewähren**
Yield

**Anlieger frei**
Residents only

**Baustelle**
Roadwork

**gefährliche Kurve**
Dangerous curve

**Unterkunft** •
accommodation

**Ich habe ein Zimmer reserviert**
I have a reservation

**Wo ist der Speisesaal?**
Where is the dining room?

**Wann gibt es Frühstück?**
What time is breakfast?

**Ich bin um...Uhr wieder da**
I'll be back at... o'clock

**Ich reise morgen ab**
I'm leaving tomorrow

**Essen und Trinken**
• eating and drinking

**Zum Wohl!**
Cheers!

**Es ist köstlich/scheußlich**
It's delicious/awful

**Ich trinke/rauche nicht**
I don't drink/smoke

**Ich esse kein Fleisch**
I don't eat meat

**Nichts mehr, danke**
No more for me, thank you

**Könnte ich noch etwas mehr haben?**
May I have some more?

**Wir möchten bitte zahlen?**
May we have the check?

**Ich hätte gerne eine Quittung**
Can I have a receipt?

**der Raucherbereich**
Smoking area

**die Gusundheit** •
health

**Ich fühle mich nicht wohl**
I don't feel well

**Mir ist schlecht**
I feel sick

**Wird er/sie sich wieder erholen?**
Will he/she be all right?

**Es tut hier weh**
It hurts here

**Ich habe Fieber**
I have a fever

**Ich bin im...Monat schwanger**
I'm...months pregnant

**Ich brauche ein Rezept für...**
I need a prescription for...

**Ich nehme normalerweise...**
I normally take...

**Ich bin allergisch gegen...**
I'm allergic to...

# deutsches register • German index

deutsch

## A

deutsch

deutsch

**deutsch**

**deutsch**

deutsch

deutsch

deutsch

deutsch

deutsch

deutsch

deutsch

# englisches register • English index

bandage 47
Bangladesh 318
banister 59
bank 96, 284
bank charge 96
bank transfer 96
bar 150, 152, 250, 256, 311
barb 244
Barbados 314
barbecue grill 267
barber 39, 188
bar code 106
bar counter 150
bark 296
barley 130, 184
bar mitzvah 26
barn 182
Baroque 301
barrier 298
bars 74
bar snacks 151
bar stool 150
bartender 150, 191
basalt 288
base 164
baseball 228
baseline 230
baseman 228
basement 58
base station 99
basil 133
basket 95, 106, 207, 226
basketball 226
basketball player 226
basket of fruit 126
bass clarinet 257
bass clef 256
bass guitar 258
bassinet 74
bassoon 257
bat 225, 228, 290
bat v 225, 229
bath mat 72
bathrobe 31, 73
bathroom 72
bath towel 73
bathtub 72
baton 235, 256
batsman 225
batter 228
batteries 260
battery 167, 202
battery pack 78
battleship 215
bay leaf 133
beach 264
beach bag 264
beach ball 265
beach hut 264
beach towel 265
beach umbrella 264

beak 293
beaker 167
beam 186, 235
beans 144
bean sprout 122
bear 291
beat 259
beautiful 321
beauty 105
beauty treatments 41
be born v 26
bed 70
bed and breakfast 101
bedding 74
bed linen 71
bedroom 70
bedside lamp 70
bedspread 70
bedspring 71
bee 295
beech 296
beef 118
beer 145, 151
beer tap 150
beet 125
beetle 295
before 320
beginning 321
behind 320
Belarus 316
Belgium 316
Belize 314
bell 197
below 320
belt 32, 36, 236
bench 250, 262
Benin 317
berry 296
beside 320
bet 273
better 321
between 320
beyond 320
Bhutan 318
biathlon 247
bib 30
bicep curl 251
biceps 16
bicycle 206
bidet 72
biennial 86
bifocal 51
big toe 15
bike lane 206
bike rack 207
bikini 264
binder 173
binoculars 281
biology 162
biplane 211
birch 296
birds 292
bird-watching 263

birth 52
birth certificate 26
birthday 27
birthday cake 141
birthday candles 141
birthday party 27
birth weight 53
bishop 272
bit 242
bit brace 78
bite 46
bite v 245
bitter 124, 145
black 39, 272, 274, 321
black belt 237
blackberry 127
black coffee 148
black currant 127
black-eyed peas 131
black hole 280
black olive 143
black pudding 157
Black Sea 313
black tea 149
bladder 20
blade 60, 66, 78, 89
blanket 71, 74
blazer 33
bleach 77
blender 66
blister 46
block 237
block v 227
block of flats 59
blonde 39
blood pressure 44
blood test 48
blouse 34
blow-dry v 38
blow-dryer 38
blowhole 290
blow out v 141
blue 274
bluebells 297
blueberry 127
blue cheese 136
blues 259
blush 40
board 241
board v 217
board games 272
boarding pass 213
boardwalk 265
bob 39
bobbin 276
bobby pins 38
bobsled 247
body 12
body lotion 73
bodysuit 30
bodywork 202
boil v 67

bok choy 123
Bolivia 315
bollard 214
bolt 59
bomber 211
bone 17, 119, 121
boned 121
bone meal 88
bongos 257
book 168
book a flight v 212
bookshelf 63, 168
bookstore 115
boom 95, 240
booster 281
boot 37
booties 30
bored 25
boring 321
borrow v 168
Bosnia and
    Herzegovina 316
Botswana 317
bottle 61, 75, 135, 311
bottled water 144
bottle opener 68, 150
bottom tier 141
boundary line 225
bouquet 35, 111
bouquet garni 132
bout 237
boutique 115
bow 240, 249
bowl 61, 65, 112
bowl v 225
bowler 225
bowling 249
bowling ball 249
bow tie 36
box 254
boxercise 251
boxer shorts 33
box file 173
boxing 236
boxing gloves 237
boxing ring 237
box of chocolates 113
box office 255
box of tissues 70
boy 23
boyfriend 24
bra 35
braces 50
bracelet 36
braid 39
brain 19
brake 200, 204, 206
brake v 207
brake block 207
brake fluid reservoir 202
brake lever 207
brake pedal 205

bran 130
branch 296
branch manager 96
brandy 145
brass 257
Brazil 315
Brazil nut 129
bread 157
breadcrumbs 139
bread flour 139
breadfruit 124
bread knife 68
break a record v 234
breakdown 203
breakfast 64, 156
breakfast buffet 156
breakfast cereals 107
breakfast table 156
breakfast tray 101
break water v 52
breast 12, 119
breastbone 17
breastfeed v 53
breast pump 53
breaststroke 239
breathing 47
breech birth 52
brick 187
bridge 15, 214, 258, 273, 300
bridle 242
bridle path 263
Brie 142
briefcase 37
briefs 33
brioche 157
broad beans 131
broadcast 179
broadcast v 178
broccoli 123
brochures 96
broil v 67
bronze 235
brooch 36
broom 77
broth 158
brother 22
brother-in-law 23
browband 242
brown 274
brown bread 139
brown flour 138
brown lentils 131
brown rice 130
browse v 177
browser 177
bruise 46
Brunei 319
brunette 39
brush 38, 40, 77, 83, 274
brush v 38, 50
Brussels sprout 123

english

english

english

english

english

english

english

english

english

english

english

english

english

english

english

english

# Dank • acknowledgments

DORLING KINDERSLEY would like to thank Sanjay Chauhan, Jomin Johny, Christine Lacey, Mahua Mandal, Tracey Miles, and Sonakshi Singh for design assistance, Georgina Garner for editorial and administrative help, Polly Boyd, Sonia Gavira, Nandini Gupta, Tina Jindal, Nishtha Kapil, Smita Mathur, Antara Moitra, Cathy Meeus, Isha Sharma, Nisha Shaw, and Janashree Singha for editorial help, Claire Bowers for compiling the DK picture credits, Nishwan Rasool for picture research, and Suruchi Bhatia, Maasoom Dhillon, and William Jones for app development and creation.

The publisher would like to thank the following for their kind permission to reproduce their photographs:

Abbreviations key: a-above; b-below/bottom; c-center; f-far; l-left; r-right; t-top)

**123RF.com:** Andriy Popov 34tl; Brad Wynnyk 172bc; Daniel Ernst 179tc; Hongqi Zhang 24cla. 175cr; Ingvar Bjork 60c; Kobby Dagan 259c; leonardo255 269c; Liubov Vadimovna (Luba) Nel 39cla; Ljupco Smokovski 75crb; Oleksandr Marynchenko 60bl; Olga Popova 33c; oneblink 49bc; Robert Churchill 94c; Roman Gorielov 33bc; Ruslan Kudrin 35bc, 35br; Subbotina 39cra; Sutichak Yachaingkham 39tc; Tarzhanova 37tc; Vitaly Valua 39tl; Wavebreak Media Ltd 188bl; Wilawan Khasawong 75cb; **Action Plus:** 224bc; **Alamy Images:** 154t; A.T. Willett 287bcl; Alex Segre 105ca, 195cl; Ambrophoto 24ca; Blend Images 168cr; Cultura RM 33r; Doug Houghton 107fbr; Hugh Threlfall 35tl; 176tr; Ian Allenden 48br; Ian Dagnall 270t; Ievgen Chepil 250bc; imagebroker 199tl, 249c; keith morris 178c; Martyn Evans 210b; MBI 175tl; Michael Burrell 213cra; Michael Foyle 184bl; Oleksiy Maksymenko 105tc; Paul Weston 168br; Prisma Bildagentur AG 246b; Radharc Images 197tr; RBtravel 112tl; Ruslan Kudrin 176tl; Sasa Huzjak 258t; Sergey Kravchenko 37ca; Sergio Azenha 270bc; Stanca Sanda (iPad is a trademark of Apple Inc., registered in the U.S. and other countries) 176bc; Stock Connection 287bcr; tarczas 35cr; vitaly suprun 176cl; Wavebreak Media ltd 39cl, 174b, 175tr; **Allsport/Getty Images:** 238cl; **Alvey and Towers:** 209 acr, 215bcl, 215bcr, 241cr; **Peter Anderson:** 188cbr, 271br.

**Anthony Blake Photo Library:** Charlie Stebbings 114cl; John Sims 114tcl; **Andyalte:** 98t; **Arcaid:** John Edward Linden 301bl; Martine Hamilton Knight, Architects: Chapman Taylor Partners, 213cl; Richard Bryant 301br; **Argos:** 41tcl, 66cbl, 66cl, 66br, 66bcl, 69cl, 70bcl, 71t, 77tl, 269tc, 270tl; **Axiom:** Eitan Simanor 105bcr; Ian Cumming 104; Vicki Couchman 148cr; **Beken Of Cowes Ltd:** 215cbc; **Bosch:** 76tcr, 76tc, 76tcl; **Camera Press:** 38tr, 256t, 257cr; Barry J. Holmes 148tr; Jane Hanger 159cr; Mary Germanou 259bc; **Corbis:** 78b; Anna Clopet 247tr; Ariel Skelley / Blend Images 52l; Bettmann 181tl, 181tr; Blue Jean Images 48bl; Bo Zauders 156t; Bob

Rowan 152bl; Bob Winsett 247cbl; Brian Bailey 247br; Chris Rainer 247ctl; Craig Aurness 215bl; David H.Wells 249cbr; Dennis Marsico 274bl; Dimitri Lundt 236bc; Duomo 211tl; Gail Mooney 277ctcr; George Lepp 248c; Gerald Nowak 239b; Gunter Marx 248cr; Jack Hollingsworth 231bl; Jacqui Hurst 277cbr; James L. Amos 247bl, 191ctr, 220bcr; Jan Butchofsky 277cbc; Johnathan Blair 243cr; Jose F. Poblete 191br; Jose Luis Pelaez.Inc 153tc; Karl Weatherly 220bl, 247tcr; Kelly Mooney Photography 259tl; Kevin Fleming 249bc; Kevin R. Morris 105tr, 243tl, 243tc; Kim Sayer 249tcr; Lynn Goldsmith 258t; Macduff Everton 231bcl; Mark Gibson 249bl; Mark L. Stephenson 249tcl; Michael Pole 115tr; Michael S. Yamashita 247cctcl; Mike King 247cbl; Neil Rabinowitz 214br; Pablo Corral 115bc; Paul A. Saunders 169br, 249ctcl; Paul J. Sutton 224c, 224br; Phil Schermeister 227b, 248tr; R. W Jones 309; Richard Morrell 189bc; Rick Doyle 241ctr; Robert Holmes 97br, 277ctc; Roger Ressmeyer 169tr; Russ Schleipman 229; The Purcell Team 211ctr; Vince Streano 194t; Wally McNamee 220br, 220bcl, 224bl; Wavebreak Media LTD 191bc; Yann Arhus-Bertrand 249tl; **Demetrio Carrasco / Dorling Kindersley (c) Herge / Les Editions Casterman:** 112cl; **Dorling Kindersley:** Banbury Museum 35c; Five Napkin Burger 152t; **Dixons:** 270cl, 270cr, 270bl, 270bcl, 270bcr, 270ccr; **Dreamstime.com:** Alexander Podshivalov 179tr, 191cr; Alexxl66 268tl; Andersastphoto 176tc; Andrey Popov 191bl; Arne9001 190tl; Chaoss 26c; Designsstock 269cl; Monkey Business Images 26clb; Paul Michael Hughes 162tr; Serghei Starus 190bc; **Education Photos:** John Walmsley 26tl; **Empics Ltd:** Adam Day 236br; Andy Heading 243c; Steve White 249cbc; **Getty Images:** 48bcl, 100t, 114bc, 154bl, 287tr; 94tr; David Leahy 162tl; Don Farrall / Digital Vision 176c; Ethan Miller 270bl; Inti St Clair 179bl; Liam Norris 188br; Sean Justice / Digital Vision 24br; **Dennis Gilbert:** 106tc; **Hulsta:** 70t; **Ideal Standard Ltd:** 72r; **The Image Bank/Getty Images:** 58; **Impact Photos:** Eliza Armstrong 115cr; Philip Achache 246t; **The Interior Archive:** Henry Wilson, Alfie's Market 114bl; Luke White, Architect: David Mikhail, 59tl; Simon Upton, Architect: Phillippe Starck, St Martins Lane Hotel 100bcl, 100br; **iStockphoto.com:** asterix0597 163tl; EdStock 190br; RichLegg 26bc; SorinVidis 27cr; **Jason Hawkes Aerial Photography:** 216t; **Dan Johnson:** 35r; **Kos Pictures Source:** 215cbl, 240tc, 240tr; David Williams 216b; **Lebrecht Collection:** Kate Mount 169bc; **MP Visual.com:** Mark Swallow 202t; **NASA:** 280cr, 280ccl, 281tl; **P&O Princess Cruises:** 214bl; **P A Photos:** 181br; **The Photographers' Library:** 186bl, 186bc, 186t; **Plain and Simple Kitchens:** 66t; **Powerstock Photolibrary:** 169tl, 256t, 287tc; **PunchStock:** Image Source 195tr; **Rail Images:** 208c, 208 cbl, 209br;

**Red Consultancy:** Odeon cinemas 257br; **Redferns:** 259br; Nigel Crane 259c; **Rex Features:** 106br, 259tc, 259tr, 259bl, 280b; Charles Ommaney 114tcr; J.F.F Whitehead 243cl; Patrick Barth 101tl; Patrick Frilet 189cbl; Scott Wiseman 287bl; **Royalty Free Images:** Getty Images/Eyewire 154bl; **Science & Society Picture Library:** Science Museum 202b; **Science Photo Library:** IBM Research 190cla; NASA 281cr; **SuperStock:** Ingram Publishing 62; Juanma Aparicio / age fotostock 172t; Nordic Photos 269tl; **Skyscan:** 168t, 182c, 298; Quick UK Ltd 212; **Sony:** 268bc; **Robert Streeter:** 154br; **Neil Sutherland:** 82tr, 83tl, 90t, 118, 188ctr, 196tl, 196tr, 299tl, 299bl; **The Travel Library:** Stuart Black 264t; **Travelex:** 97cl; **Vauxhall:** Technik 198t, 199tl, 199tr, 199cl, 199cr, 199ctctl, 199ctcr, 199tcl, 199tcr, 200; **View Pictures:** Dennis Gilbert, Architects: ACDP Consulting, 106t; Dennis Gilbert, Chris Wilkinson Architects, 209tr; Peter Cook, Architects: Nicholas Crimshaw and partners, 208t; **Betty Walton:** 185br; **Colin Walton:** 2, 4, 7, 9, 10, 28, 42, 56, 92, 95c, 99tl, 99tcl, 102, 116, 120t, 138t, 146, 150t, 160, 170, 191ctcl, 192, 218, 252, 260br, 260l, 261tr, 261c, 261cr, 271ctbl, 271cbr, 271ctl, 278, 287br, 302, 401.

DK PICTURE LIBRARY:

Akhil Bahkshi; Patrick Baldwin; Geoff Brightling; British Museum; John Bulmer; Andrew Butler; Joe Cornish; Brian Cosgrove; Andy Crawford and Kit Hougton; Philip Dowell; Alistair Duncan; Gables; Bob Gathany; Norman Hollands; Kew Gardens; Peter James Kindersley; Vladimir Kozlik; Sam Lloyd; London Northern Bus Company Ltd; Tracy Morgan; David Murray and Jules Selmes; Musée Vivant du Cheval, France; Museum of Broadcast Communications; Museum of Natural History; NASA; National History Museum; Norfolk Rural Life Museum; Stephen Oliver; RNLI; Royal Ballet School; Guy Ryecart; Science Museum; Neil Setchfield; Ross Simms and the Winchcombe Folk Police Museum; Singapore Symphony Orchestra; Smart Museum of Art; Tony Souter; Erik Svensson and Jeppe Wikstrom; Sam Tree of Kevgrove Marketing Ltd; Barrie Watts; Alan Williams; Jerry Young.

Additional photography by Colin Walton.

Colin Walton would like to thank:
A&A News, Uckfield; Abbey Music, Tunbridge Wells; Arena Mens Clothing, Tunbridge Wells; Burrells of Tunbridge Wells; Gary at Di Marco's; Jeremy's Home Store, Tunbridge Wells; Noakes of Tunbridge Wells; Ottakar's, Tunbridge Wells; Selby's of Uckfield; Sevenoaks Sound and Vision; Westfield, Royal Victoria Place, Tunbridge Wells.

All other images © Dorling Kindersley
For further information see: www.dkimages.com

deutsch • english